To mark his 80th birthday on 28 October 2010,
I would like to dedicate this book to Bernie Ecclestone
in recognition of his unflagging support of my work
and all that he has done for the sport we all love so much.

Rainer W. Schlegelmilch

THE GOLDEN AGE OF FORMULA 1

Text by Hartmut Lehbrink

teNeues

Foreword by Sir Jackie Stewart

I have been very fortunate to be a part of the golden years of Formula 1 grand prix racing, in the beginning as an autograph hunter and enthusiast, and later on as a grand prix driver. For me, though, the golden age has ranged from that first world championship Formula 1 race at Silverstone in 1950 to the races that I still attend in this, the 21st century.

In the fifties, Italy was the capital for motor sport, not just because of the Italian Grand Prix at Monza, which is a very special event, but also because of "the Big Three", Alfa Romeo, Ferrari and Maserati, as well as the Italian manufacturing companies who supported them. That remained the case until two British gentlemen, John Cooper and Colin Chapman, came along and put the engines in the middle of the car behind the driver. Cooper, Lotus and the Coventry Climax engine started bringing world championships to Great Britain, triggering a development that was to make the country the hub of the motor racing world.

In the early days of sports television, very little coverage was given to the Formula 1 cars in their national colours. However this changed as cars became branded with tobacco companies and cosmetic manufacturers, who blazoned the trail of recognition for Formula 1 racing to become the largest capital investment sport in the world, attracting the biggest sports television audience on an annual basis around our planet. The technology of the sport changed dramatically. An increasing financial commitment brought new dimensions to the research and development of engineering and new materials, such as the world had never previously seen, other than within the aerospace industry.

However, the human element has not changed at all in my opinion. The "animal" (the driver), is the same today, with exactly the same mentality as those who were racing yesteryear, such as Farina, Ascari and Fangio in the fifties. Today we have a wonderful collection of drivers who are as skilled and as talented as I think there has ever been in the history of Formula 1. We have a bigger audience who are intoxicated by the cars and their stars. The demographics of Formula 1 are so impressive that it attracts people and nationalities from every station in life.

The glamour and the excitement that the golden age of Formula 1 once provided is as true today as it ever has been. The racing drivers, designers, aerodynamicists and technicians receive colossal fees to demonstrate their skills. Consumer products of multi-national corporations utilise Formula 1, in search of corporate identity and multi-national sales.

Formula 1 has been responsible for probably the best example of risk management of any business, corporation or sport throughout the world, recovering from a period in the late sixties and early seventies, where death became a constant companion to the world of grand prix racing. Formula 1 is now a global anomaly; it is *countries* who desire a grand prix, not a track owner or an automobile club. Governments and heads of state want to showcase their region, their country or their state around the world in the most positive light.

The army of journalists, television crews, commentators and photographers who project Formula 1 races around the world have also accelerated the technology they bring with them. Rainer Schlegelmilch has experienced this and has been part of the development in his field. The cameras he uses today, with their many lenses festooned around his body, record the images in greater focus, more vivid colours, higher definition and clarity than his equipment of past years.

The sport has changed and it has been for the good. The more favourable elements remain, as do the best people. I have a belief that if you are going to become successful, first you have to have experience, and from experience you gain knowledge, and from both of them, you can hopefully enjoy wisdom. Finally, some may get maturity. Rainer Schlegelmilch has all of those attributes; he is producing better photographs today than he has ever done in his long career in motor sports. He's one of the best known people in the business and is highly respected.

Rainer's composition has developed into an art of the highest level. That is why he has been able to represent the golden age of Formula 1 in its most graphic and stylish form and this book truly showcases all of those great years, great cars and great people.

Vorwort von Sir Jackie Stewart

Es war mein großes Glück, am Goldenen Zeitalter der Formel 1 teilhaben zu dürfen, anfangs als Autogrammjäger und begeisterter Fan und später als Fahrer. Für mich beginnt jedoch das Goldene Zeitalter mit dem ersten Formel-1-Weltmeisterschaftslauf in Silverstone im Jahr 1950, und dauert an bis zu den Rennen, die ich auch jetzt, im 21. Jahrhundert, noch besuche.

In den Fünfzigern war Italien das Mekka des Motorsports, nicht nur wegen des Grand Prix von Monza, einer ganz besonderen Veranstaltung, sondern auch wegen der „Großen Drei", Alfa Romeo, Ferrari und Maserati, und wegen der italienischen Hersteller, die sie unterstützten. Das blieb so bis zum Erscheinen zweier englischer Gentlemen, John Cooper und Colin Chapman. Sie bauten das Triebwerk in der Mitte des Wagens ein, direkt hinter dem Fahrer. Cooper, Lotus und der Coventry-Climax-Motor brachten die Weltmeisterschaft nach Großbritannien. So wurde der Grundstein für eine Entwicklung gelegt, die das Vereinigte Königreich zum Zentrum des Motorsports machte.

Zu Beginn des Sportfernsehens stand die Formel 1 mit ihren Fahrzeugen in Nationalfarben nur sehr selten auf dem Programm. Das änderte sich allerdings, als die Wagen zunehmend mit den Logos von Tabak- und Kosmetikunternehmen versehen wurden. Diese Konzerne sorgten dafür, dass sich die Formel 1 als anerkannter Sport etablierte, der weltweit die meisten Investitionen anzieht und der Jahr um Jahr im Fernsehen die höchsten Zuschauerzahlen auf dem gesamten Erdball zu verzeichnen hat. Die Technologie dieses Sports hat sich rasant verändert. Mit zunehmenden, gesicherten Investitionen eröffneten sich neue Dimensionen der Forschung, und so wurde eine Entwicklung der Technik sowie neuer Materialien ermöglicht, welche die Welt vorher nur aus der Luft- und Raumfahrtindustrie kannte.

Die menschliche Komponente hat sich meines Erachtens trotzdem überhaupt nicht verändert. Im Mittelpunkt steht immer noch das „Tier" (der Fahrer), mit genau der gleichen Mentalität wie diejenigen, die damals Rennen gefahren sind, wie zum Beispiel Farina, Ascari und Fangio in den Fünfzigern. Ich denke, die Fahrer von heute sind talentierter und besser ausgebildet, als es je eine Generation in der Geschichte der Formel 1 war. Wir haben eine größere Fangemeinde, die von den Wagen und den Stars fasziniert ist. Die Zusammensetzung des Publikums ist sehr beeindruckend. Eine heterogene Gruppe von Menschen aus aller Welt fühlt sich von der Formel 1 angezogen.

Auch der Glanz und die Spannung, die schon das Goldene Zeitalter der Formel 1 ausmachten, sind heute präsent wie eh und je. Rennfahrer, Designer, Aerodynamiker und Techniker, sie alle werden hervorragend bezahlt, um ihr Können zur Verfügung zu stellen. Multinationale Konzerne benutzen die Formel 1, um ihre Produkte zu vermarkten, ihre Corporate Identity zu stärken und den internationalen Markt zu erobern.

Die Formel 1 ist weltweit das wahrscheinlich beste Beispiel in Bezug auf Risiko-Management in den Bereichen Wirtschaft und Sport. Sie hat sich von der schwierigen Phase der späten sechziger und frühen siebziger Jahre erholt, in welcher der Tod ein ständiger Begleiter der Grand-Prix-Rennen war. Die Formel 1 stellt heute eine weltweite Ausnahmeerscheinung dar: Es sind die *Länder*, die einen Grand Prix ausrichten wollen, nicht die Rennstrecken-Betreiber oder die Automobilclubs. Regierungen oder Regierungschefs wollen ihre Region oder ihr Land auf bestmögliche Weise global präsentieren.

Die vielen Journalisten, Fernsehcrews, Kommentatoren und Fotografen, mit deren Hilfe die Formel 1 in die gesamte Welt übertragen wird, arbeiten heute ebenfalls mit verbesserter Technologie. Rainer Schlegelmilch hat diese Entwicklung aus nächster Nähe miterlebt und war selbst an den Neuerungen in diesem Bereich beteiligt. Die Kameras, die er heute einsetzt, und die vielen Objektive, die er mit sich herumträgt, sorgen für noch schärfere Aufnahmen, erzeugen viel lebhaftere Farben, eine höhere Auflösung und Klarheit als seine frühere Ausrüstung.

Der Sport hat sich verändert, und das zu seinem Besten. Die besseren Elemente bleiben erhalten, so wie auch die besten Leute. Ich glaube, dass es zum Erfolg zunächst einmal Erfahrung braucht. Aus der Erfahrung gewinnt man Erkenntnis und aus beiden vielleicht sogar Weisheit. Manchen gelingt es schließlich auch, zur Reife zu gelangen. Rainer Schlegelmilch vereinigt all das in sich – er macht heute bessere Fotografien als jemals zuvor in seiner langen Karriere als Motorsport-Fotograf. Er gehört zu den bekanntesten Personen des Geschäfts und ist hoch angesehen.

Rainers Kompositionen haben sich zu Kunst auf höchstem Niveau entwickelt. Ihm ist es gelungen, das Goldene Zeitalter der Formel 1 auf elegante und anschauliche Weise abzubilden, so dass dieser Band zu einem beeindruckenden Zeugnis einer besonderen Ära voller großartiger Rennwagen und Persönlichkeiten wird.

Préface de Sir Jackie Stewart

J'ai eu l'immense chance de vivre pleinement l'âge d'or des Grands Prix de Formule 1, au départ en tant que chasseur d'autographes et passionné et plus tard en tant que pilote de Grand Prix. Cependant, cet âge d'or s'étend selon moi de la première course de Championnat du monde de Formule 1 à Silverstone en 1950 aux courses du 21e siècle, que je continue de suivre.

Pendant les années cinquante, l'Italie fut la capitale du sport automobile grâce au Grand Prix de Monza, un événement exceptionnel, mais surtout grâce aux « Trois Grands », Alfa Romeo, Ferrari et Maserati et aux fabricants italiens qui leur apportaient leur soutien. Il en fut ainsi jusqu'à ce que deux Britanniques, John Cooper et Colin Chapman, ne les rattrapent avec leurs moteurs centraux placés derrière le pilote. Grâce à Cooper, Lotus et au moteur Coventry Climax, la Grande-Bretagne commença à remporter des championnats du monde, enclenchant ainsi un processus qui n'allait pas tarder à faire de ce pays la pierre angulaire de la course automobile mondiale.

Aux débuts de la télévision sportive, très peu d'attention était accordée aux formules 1 arborant les couleurs nationales. Cependant, la situation évolua lorsque les bolides commencèrent à afficher des marques de tabac et de cosmétiques. Les Grands Prix de Formule 1 acquirent une reconnaissance légitime et la Formule 1 devint le sport attirant le plus d'investissements et atteignant la plus forte audience de sport à la télévision, sur une base annuelle au niveau mondial. La technologie inhérente à ce sport changea radicalement. Une augmentation des engagements financiers apporta une nouvelle dimension à la recherche et au développement de la technique et des nouveaux matériaux, une évolution sans précédent, si l'on ne tient compte de celle qu'a connue l'industrie aérospatiale.

Toutefois, je pense que l'élément humain n'a absolument pas changé. L' « animal » (le pilote) d'aujourd'hui est le même que celui d'hier, il possède exactement la même mentalité que les pilotes ayant couru autrefois, tels que Farina, Ascari et Fangio dans les années cinquante. Aujourd'hui, nous avons une pléiade de pilotes d'une habileté et d'un talent selon moi jamais vu auparavant dans l'histoire de la Formule 1. Notre public, fasciné par les bolides et leurs stars, s'est élargi. Les chiffres de la Formule 1 sont véritablement impressionnants car ce sport attire toutes les nationalités et toutes les tranches d'âge.

Le glamour et la fièvre générés par la Formule 1 durant son âge d'or n'ont pas perdu une once d'intensité. Les pilotes de course, designers, aérodynamiciens et techniciens perçoivent des sommes colossales pour démontrer leurs compétences. Les produits de consommation de multinationales se servent de la Formule 1 pour forger leur image de marque et doper leurs ventes au niveau mondial.

Parmi les différentes activités commerciales, corporations ou autres sports, la Formule 1 a été et demeure probablement un modèle en matière de gestion du risque, et ce au niveau mondial. Après la fin des années soixante, début des années soixante-dix, période durant laquelle la mort s'abattait trop souvent sur les Grands Prix, la Formule 1 a su se rétablir avec brio. La Formule 1 est une exception internationale, ce sont les *pays* qui désirent un Grand Prix et non un propriétaire de circuit ou bien une écurie. Les gouvernements et les chefs d'État souhaitent bénéficier d'une vitrine pour y présenter leur région, leur pays ou leur État au monde entier, sous le plus bel angle qui soit.

L'armada de journalistes, équipes de télévision, commentateurs et photographes qui présentent les courses de Formule 1 à travers le monde entier sont également à la pointe en matière de technologie. Rainer Schlegelmilch a suivi cette évolution au plus près et a contribué aux avancées dans son domaine. Avec les différents objectifs qu'il a toujours sur lui, les appareils photo qu'il utilise aujourd'hui produisent des images bien plus nettes, d'une plus haute définition et clarté et des couleurs plus vives que le matériel utilisé par le passé.

Le sport a changé et en bien. Les meilleurs éléments restent, les meilleures personnalités aussi. Je pense que si tu désires connaître la réussite, tu dois commencer par avoir de l'expérience et de cette expérience, tu acquiers des connaissances et grâce à ces deux éléments, tu peux, espérons-le du moins, profiter de ton savoir. Au final, certains ont la chance d'acquérir de la maturité. Rainer Schlegelmilch possède tous ces atouts; il réalise aujourd'hui les meilleures photographies de sa longue carrière dans le sport automobile. Il est l'une des personnalités les plus réputées dans ce domaine et est hautement respecté.

L'œuvre de Rainer a atteint le plus haut niveau de son art. Il a véritablement su présenter l'âge d'or de la Formule 1 dans sa forme la plus graphique et stylée. Cet ouvrage illustre fidèlement toutes ces belles années, ces belles voitures et ces belles personnalités.

Prefacio de Sir Jackie Stewart

He tenido la gran suerte de formar parte de los años dorados de la Fórmula 1, primero como cazador de autógrafos y entusiasta, más tarde como piloto de Grandes Premios. No obstante, para mí la edad de oro se ha extendido desde aquella primera carrera del Campeonato del Mundo de Fórmula 1 en Silverstone en 1950, hasta las carreras a las que sigo asistiendo en este siglo XXI.

En los cincuenta, Italia era la capital del deporte del motor, no sólo por el Gran Premio de Italia en Monza, un evento muy especial, sino también por los "Tres Grandes", Alfa Romeo, Ferrari y Maserati, así como por los fabricantes italianos que los apoyaban. Esa situación se mantuvo hasta que llegaron dos caballeros británicos, John Cooper y Colin Chapman, y colocaron los motores en el centro del coche tras el piloto. Cooper, Lotus y el motor Coventry Climax comenzaron a ganar títulos mundiales para Gran Bretaña, provocando un desarrollo que iba a convertir el país en el centro del mundo de las carreras.

En los primeros días del deporte televisado, la cobertura dada a los coches de Fórmula 1 en sus colores nacionales era mínima. Sin embargo, esto cambió cuando los coches fueron cubiertos con marcas de tabaco y cosméticos, que iniciaron la popularización de la Fórmula 1 hasta convertirse en el deporte con mayor inversión de capital del mundo, el de mayores audiencias televisivas anuales del planeta. La tecnología del deporte cambió radicalmente. Gracias al mayor flujo de capital, la investigación y el desarrollo de la ingeniería y los nuevos materiales alcanzaron dimensiones nunca vistas antes, a no ser en la industria aeroespacial.

Aun así, creo que el factor humano no ha cambiado del todo. El "animal" (el piloto), es el mismo hoy y tiene exactamente la misma mentalidad que sus colegas de antaño, como Farina, Ascari y Fangio en los cincuenta. Hoy tenemos una estupenda colección de pilotos, en mi opinión tan hábil y talentosa como ninguna otra generación en la historia de la Fórmula 1. Tenemos un público mucho mayor, embriagado por los coches y sus estrellas. La diversidad en la Fórmula 1 es tan impresionante que atrae a personas y nacionalidades de cualquier edad y condición.

El encanto y la excitación proporcionados una vez por la era de oro de la Fórmula 1 son tan auténticos hoy como no lo han sido nunca. Los pilotos, diseñadores, ingenieros aerodinámicos y técnicos reciben colosales honorarios para mostrar sus habilidades. Los productos de las multinacionales utilizan la Fórmula 1, en busca de una identidad corporativa y ventas a nivel mundial.

La Fórmula 1 ha sido responsable del que probablemente sea el mejor ejemplo de gestión de riesgo de cualquier negocio, empresa o deporte del mundo, reponiéndose de un periodo, entre finales de los sesenta y principios de los setenta, en el que la muerte se convirtió en un compañero habitual del mundo de los Grandes Premios. Ahora mismo, la Fórmula 1 es una anomalía global; son los *países* los que desean un Gran Premio, no el dueño de un circuito o un club de automovilistas. Gobiernos y jefes de estado quieren mostrar al mundo su región, su país o su estado de la forma más positiva posible.

La tecnología que porta el ejército de periodistas, equipos de televisión, comentadores y fotógrafos que transmiten las carreras de Fórmula 1 por todo el mundo también ha acelerado. Rainer Schlegelmilch ha vivido esto y ha formado parte del desarrollo en este campo. Las cámaras que usa hoy, con sus objetivos adornando su cuerpo, capturan imágenes con un enfoque fantástico, con colores más vivos, mayor definición y claridad que su equipo de años pasados.

El deporte ha cambiado y lo ha hecho a mejor. Los elementos más favorables se mantienen, como lo hacen las mejores personas. Tengo el convencimiento de que si quieres tener éxito, primero debes tener experiencia, de la experiencia adquieres conocimiento, y mediante ambos tal vez poseas sabiduría. Finalmente, puede que algunos alcancen la madurez. Rainer Schlegelmilch tiene todos estos atributos; sus fotografías actuales son las mejores de su larga carrera en el mundo del motor. Es una de las personas más conocidas en el negocio y goza de gran respeto.

El trabajo de Rainer se ha convertido en un arte en su máxima expresión. Realmente ha logrado plasmar La Edad de Oro de la Fórmula 1 en su forma más gráfica y elegante y este libro capta con total fidelidad la esencia de todos esos maravillosos años, grandes coches y estupendos personajes.

Prefazione di Sir Jackie Stewart

Mi ritengo molto fortunato ad aver vissuto gli anni d'oro delle corse di Formula 1, all'inizio come semplice appassionato a caccia di autografi e più tardi come pilota nelle gare del Gran Premio. Questo periodo magico, che per me ha avuto inizio da quel primo Campionato Mondiale disputato a Silverstone, nel 1950, continua ancora oggi, nella realtà automobilistica del XXI secolo di cui ancora faccio parte.

Negli anni cinquanta l'Italia era la capitale dello sport motoristico, non solo per via del Gran Premio di Monza, ma anche in virtù delle "Tre Grandi" di quegli anni – Alfa Romeo, Ferrari e Maserati – e delle case automobilistiche italiane che le finanziavano. Così è stato fino a quando dalla collaborazione nata tra due inglesi, John Cooper e Colin Chapman, si arrivò alla reintroduzione del motore posteriore, al centro della vettura, dietro al pilota. Grazie a Cooper, a Lotus e al motore Coventry Climax, la Gran Bretagna vinse i suoi primi Campionati Mondiali, innescando una fase di sviluppo che avrebbe fatto di questo paese il cuore dell'automobilismo mondiale.

La televisione sportiva degli esordi dava pochissimo spazio ai colori nazionali delle automobili in gara. Poi le cose sono cambiate e si è cominciato a imprimere sulle vetture i marchi delle principali multinazionali del tabacco e delle grandi case cosmetiche, che hanno riconosciuto l'importanza dell'identificazione con il mondo delle corse di Formula 1 facendole diventare il principale settore d'investimento in ambito sportivo a livello mondiale, oltre che l'evento televisivo più seguito in tutto il pianeta. Ciò ha determinato un cambiamento radicale nella tecnologia del settore automobilistico.

Credo tuttavia che il fattore umano non sia per nulla cambiato. L'"animale" (il pilota) è lo stesso di ieri e il suo modo di ragionare è il medesimo di quelli che hanno corso prima di lui, personaggi come Farina, Ascari e Fangio, che fecero grande l'automobilismo degli anni cinquanta. Oggi abbiamo uno straordinario campionario di piloti, che possiedono talenti e abilità come credo ve ne siano sempre stati nella storia della Formula 1. Abbiamo un pubblico più vasto, inebriato dalle automobili e dalle stelle del volante. La demografia della Formula 1 è tale da comprendere una varietà straordinaria di persone e nazionalità di ogni appartenenza sociale.

Il glamour e l'eccitazione che hanno caratterizzato gli anni d'oro della Formula 1 oggi sono una realtà più che mai tangibile. Piloti, progettisti, aerodinamicisti e tecnici ricevono compensi enormi per dar prova della loro bravura, mentre i prodotti di consumo di una multinazionale utilizzano la Formula 1 per legare il proprio nome all'immagine dell'azienda e aumentare le vendite in tutto il mondo.

Dopo un periodo difficile tra la fine degli anni sessanta e l'inizio dei settanta – in cui la morte era diventata una presenza costante nelle corse del grande circuito automobilistico – la Formula 1 ha dimostrato di possedere ottime doti manageriali, alla stregua delle più grandi società di gestione del rischio internazionali, fino a diventare un pezzo da novanta tra le realtà sportive mondiali, oltre che un'autentica anomalia: oggi, infatti, il Gran Premio è ambito non soltanto dal proprietario di un circuito o da un club automobilistico, bensì da governi e capi di stato, che desiderano dar lustro al proprio paese fornendone al mondo un'immagine brillante e positiva.

L'esercito di giornalisti che trasmettono in tutto il mondo le immagini delle gare di Formula 1 ha contribuito ad aumentare il livello tecnologico delle apparecchiature utilizzate. Rainer Schlegelmilch ha vissuto questa trasformazione, di cui peraltro è stato uno dei protagonisti. Rispetto al passato, oggi utilizza macchine fotografiche dotate di una quantità di obiettivi (li porta tutti appesi addosso) che garantiscono immagini con una migliore messa a fuoco, colori più vividi, una definizione e una limpidezza più nette.

Lo sport è cambiato ed è cambiato in meglio. Restano i fattori positivi, così come restano gli uomini migliori. Sono convinto che per ottenere successo sia necessario prima acquisire esperienza, perché da questa si maturano solide competenze e solo alla fine si può assaporare il piacere della saggezza. Alcuni raggiungono anche la piena maturità. Rainer Schlegelmilch riassume in sé ciascuna di queste caratteristiche; oggi realizza foto migliori di quante ne abbia mai scattate in tutta la sua lunga carriera nel settore degli sport motoristici ed è una delle figure più conosciute e più stimate del giro.

Le composizioni di Rainer si sono evolute fino a diventare opere d'arte di alto livello. Egli è riuscito a rappresentare l'Epoca d'Oro della Formula 1 nella sua espressione più vivida e raffinata e questo libro è una rappresentazione sincera di tutto quanto è appartenuto a quegli anni gloriosi, alle loro grandi automobili, ai loro indimenticabili protagonisti.

Formula 1 in the Sixties

A Study in *Zeitgeist*

Time is a variable. A journalist once asked Albert Einstein if he could explain his Theory of Relativity in a clear and vivid way, to which the roguish genius replied: "Imagine spending five minutes on the sofa with a beautiful woman, and five sitting naked on a blistering hotplate. Then you'll understand what I mean". The twenties was a decade that was perceived, lived and felt differently to the fifties. A grand prix makes a much deeper impression upon the way we perceive the passing of time than reading the local paper after breakfast.

But even here, we must draw a distinction. A grand prix in the first decade of the third millennium leaves a much weaker mark on our consciousness than was the case in the sixties. Just the sheer number of rounds making up today's calendar (nineteen in 2010, compared to approximately ten back then) causes our feeling of inner devotion to evaporate. At the European GP 2010, Mark Webber's Red Bull car took off into the blue Valencia sky at over 185 miles per hour, completing a summersault and finally hurtling, still at tremendous speed, into the tyre-walls. But the Australian just shook himself off, angrily throwing his high-tech steering wheel out of the cockpit. And that was basically it. Since Ayrton Senna's death on the 1st of May 1994, a new sort of airy confidence reigns. The possibility of a Formula 1 driver dying while doing his job has been erased from our minds – events seem to unfold just as if in a video game.

For Webber's high-speed predecessors half a century ago, however, things would have turned nasty. As soon as the start flag fell, danger was on the prowl. It was not a rare occurance for a black mushroom cloud on the horizon to announce a tragedy. Minutes seemed to last an eternity. On the 23rd of April 1962, motor sport brutally discharged one of its greatest, as Stirling Moss's Lotus smashed into a bank of earth on the fast Goodwood circuit. The balding acrobat at the steering wheel was later granted his retirement, turbulent as it turned out to be. "A Nodding Acquaintance with Death" became the title of one of his autobiographies. Meetings with the Grim Reaper were already familiar to the drivers, purely because they had repeatedly been eyewitnesses of others' deaths. Almost every year, he would pluck one or two victims from the line-up of twenty fearless men practising the sport at its highest level.

No wonder: the race tracks were absurdly dangerous – natural circuits like Spa-Francorchamps and the old *Nürburgring* were, in 1921 and 1927 respectively, dug out of what had been the dark coniferous forests of Ardennes and the Eifel. The hedges that lined the "Green Hell" circuit until 1970 offered about as much protection as a thick bank of cloud would give in a plane crash. And then Monaco: until the first crash barriers sprouted up out of the asphalt in the second half of the sixties, kerbstones, façades, lamps and balustrades all threatened to bring the high-speed venture there to abrupt ends. There is a gruesome irony in the fact that the crash and resulting fire, which was fatal to Lorenzo Bandini in 1967, could be directly attributed to the first, clumsy security measures that had been put in place: the bales of straw lining the harbour chicane were reinforced with poles, which were hit by the Ferrari side-on, causing a lateral rollover.

Cars in those days were fragile creatures, designed for the normal strains of a grand prix and nothing more. Sometimes they were not even up to the challenges that a "normal working day" would throw at them. "Whenever I am overtaken by a wheel of my own car, I know I must be sitting in a Lotus", Graham Hill liked to jest, and he wasn't the only one. The term "safety" was, for a long time, absent from the vocabulary of grand prix drivers. Quite the opposite – the romance of the craft seemed to derive not least from its very proximity to death. Towards the end of the decade, men like Jackie Stewart began energetically to take care of improving security measures in this frenzied work environment. The fact that drivers were now clad in increasingly effective, fire-resistant materials, and protected by full-face crash helmets, incurred nothing but the taunts and jibes of purist Stirling Moss, himself having been the victim of an accident. Here, he was heard to say, a new species of sissies and wimps was evolving, people who indeed had no business being in the sport. And one of the wild youths applauded this: Jacky Ickx.

They drove, despite the low wages, simply for the love of driving. The sixties generation was practically tireless, on the track nearly every weekend, and then appearing in more exotic arenas in the winter months, such as the Tasman Series. And their versatility made them shine, unlike the mono-talents that are now the order of the day. To give a few examples, Jim Clark, Formula 1 world champion in 1963 and 1965, also won in Indianapolis in 1965, and had great entertainment value as a touring car pilot in a Lotus Cortina. Graham Hill, in addition to his two world championship titles, in 1962 and 1968, had successes in Indy (1966) and at Le Mans (1972). Jochen Rindt, grand prix title-holder in 1970, took himself to victory on the Sarthe circuit in 1965. They called him the "King of Formula 2" – and indeed it was a point of honour for a Formula 1 driver to ride out in these small, nimble single-seaters, and a pleasant undertaking at that. Jacky Ickx, Jo Siffert and Pedro Rodriguez all proved themselves to be just as greatly gifted in grand prix motor vehicles as in sports car racing over long distances. With Mario Andretti the decade ended up producing one of the finest all-rounders that motor sport had ever seen.

The constant presence of that ultimate risk meant that protagonists of that period bonded much more closely than their successors do now, in the year 2010, protected in their adamantine cocoons of carbon fibre. In his autobiography "All Arms and Elbows", which is as funny as it is moving, Innes Ireland – always disposed to tell a joke – draws attention to the lively camaraderie of his contemporaries. While today's Formula 1 set tend to depart from the location of their latest appearance as hurriedly as if on an official engagement, travelling separately on principle

and eyeing their race-track rivals with suspicion, the older generation knew how to celebrate: they ran riot on more than one occasion. Consider such alcohol-induced states of ecstasy at the victory celebrations visited live in John Frankenheimer's famous 1966 film epic "Grand Prix". Before complete commercialization and scientification led this sport to lose a lot of its heat, the women at the tracks were given supporting roles, not just acting as ornaments in the pit and paddock, but rather recording times, keeping scoring tables and generally earning a place in the heart and soul of the man by their side.

Of course, racing in the sixties was embedded in the past and future. It evolved from the 2.5-litre period (last year 1960), whose vehicles had been inspired by the (front-engine) architecture and appearance of legendary pre-war racing cars. Only towards the end of the decade did that also go for the rear-engined "Silver Arrows", deployed into the German-German battle by the German *Auto Union*, once described by a cynic as a four metre-long motor tract with a jump seat at the front. Beginning with the three-litre era, which started rather hesitantly in 1966 and lasted until 1986, the sixties came to be intermeshed with the decades to come. A milestone was laid by the victory of Jim Clark in Zandvoort in 1967, in a Lotus 49, with the newly created compact Ford V8 DFV (for "double four valve" because of its two banks with four valves per cylinder) breathing down the driver's neck. This engine left its mark on Formula 1 for nearly twenty years, its final triumph being for Michele Alboreto in a Tyrrell, in Detroit, 1983.

The period between 1961 and 1965, featuring small and elegant cars with 1.5-litre engines, formed the very centrepiece of the sixties in terms of Formula 1. This started with Ferrari having total dominance, ran on with John Surtees' practically last-minute win in his car bearing the *cavallino rampante*, while Ferrari itself was victorious in the constructors' championship in 1964, and finished with a victory for Honda at the final race in Mexico City.

Nevertheless, it was increasingly not the Italians who held the balance of power as they had done in the fifties (their run only briefly interrupted in the years of Mercedes dominance, 1954 and 1955), but the British. The period was remarkable for its astonishing diversity and positively democratic breadth in terms of the numbers of participants. In five years and 46 grands prix, it had 101 drivers in vehicles of 21 different makes in action.

At the fore, meanwhile, the usual suspects in the usual makes of car were taking care of affairs between themselves, except when a case of extraordinary good luck arose, such as the victory of the grand prix novice Giancarlo Baghetti at the French GP in Reims, 1961. The most outstanding driver of this era was Jim Clark. Yet there were enough men to make life difficult for the Scot. After all, the sixties saw seven different world champions, including the Australian Jack Brabham – tight-lipped, determined and a remorseless opponent on the track. He was the one who brought us that famous phrase, "when the flag drops, the bullshit stops". He only really had confidence in himself, and so from 1962 began building his own cars, winning in Reims in 1966 to become the first driver ever to win a grand prix in a vehicle bearing his own name.

Then there was Phil Hill, who, in 1961, with only two wins that season, became the first American to have his name entered into the list of Formula 1 champions. He was a gentleman with a keen mind, who once arrived late to practice because he wanted to hear the end of a mass by Mozart on the car radio. There was his namesake Graham Hill, the moustached Londoner: the English Hill let his fame and reputation decline, following his second world championship title, simply because he could not bear to give up the sport. In 1975 he finally stepped down, only to be involved in a fatal plane crash in November that same year. It sounds like somebody's terrible joke. Then there was Jim Clark himself, whom many people today still consider the greatest racer of all time, although the idea that he was just a humble Scottish sheep farmer, who had strayed onto the racetrack by mistake, stubbornly clung on.

There was John Surtees who arrived from the world of motorcycle racing, "the only champion on both two and four wheels" as the public had hammered home in clichéd repetition. There was the New Zealander Denis Hulme, known as "the bear", remarkable for his stoic calm and quaint reliability. And there was Jackie Stewart, "flying Scot" number two in chronological order. Already finishing sixth in his first grand prix in East London, South Africa, in January 1965, then reaching third place at the Monaco GP five months later and winning in Monza that same year, he seemed destined for higher places. This was amply granted, as Stewart became three times champion in 1969, 1971 and 1973. Any mention of those remaining is subjective. They too – like many others – left their mark on Formula 1. The notoriously unlucky Chris Amon; the oblong American, Dan Gurney, who looked like a Viking landed in the wrong century; the bold Belgian Jacky Ickx; Bruce McLaren, New Zealander like Amon and as accomplished a driver as he was racing car designer, and the up-and-coming Jochen Rindt.

Enzo Ferrari slammed his English adversary Colin Chapman – company founder, boss and director of operations at Lotus – as a "garagist", someone who cobbled together a racing car out of series parts and a few of his own ingredients. All the same, the sixties boiled down to the duel between these two exponents with entirely different philosophies – the determined, conservative mentality of one, the ultra-progressive mindset of the other. Chapman's creations, such as the Lotus 25 of 1962 with its *monocoque* frame, revolutionized this high-speed art as much as his lucrative flash of inspiration to varnish his fleet of fast cars, from 1968 onwards, with the colours of external sponsor Gold Leaf, the cigarette brand.

1970 in many respects emerged as a transition period in the history of grand prix, becoming almost the antithesis to the ten preceding years. Formula 1 lost Bruce McLaren, Piers Courage and Jochen Rindt, who passed away, and Jack Brabham and Dan Gurney retired. The sport gained, however, young talents such as Clay Regazzoni, Emerson Fittipaldi, Ronnie Peterson and François Cevert.

The fascination remained. But the atmosphere was different.

Die Formel 1 in den sechziger Jahren
Versuch eines Stimmungsbildes

Zeit ist eine Variable. Albert Einstein wurde einmal von Journalisten gebeten, seine Relativitätstheorie auf anschauliche Weise zu erklären. „Stellen Sie sich vor", sagte der schalkhafte Genius, „Sie verbringen fünf Minuten mit einer schönen Frau auf einem Sofa oder mit dem bloßen Hintern auf einer glühenden Herdplatte. Dann werden Sie verstehen, was ich meine." Die Zwanziger wurden anders empfunden, gelebt und gefühlt als die Fünfziger. Ein Grand Prix macht sich im Zeit-Empfinden sehr viel nachdrücklicher bemerkbar als die ausgiebige Lektüre der Lokalzeitung nach dem Frühstück.

Aber selbst hier müssen wir unterscheiden. Ein Großer Preis im ersten Jahrzehnt des dritten Millenniums beansprucht die Wahrnehmung weitaus weniger intensiv, als dies in den sechziger Jahren der Fall gewesen wäre. Schon die bloße Menge von Läufen, die den Jahres-Zyklus in unserer Zeit ausmachen (2010 sind es 19 gegenüber

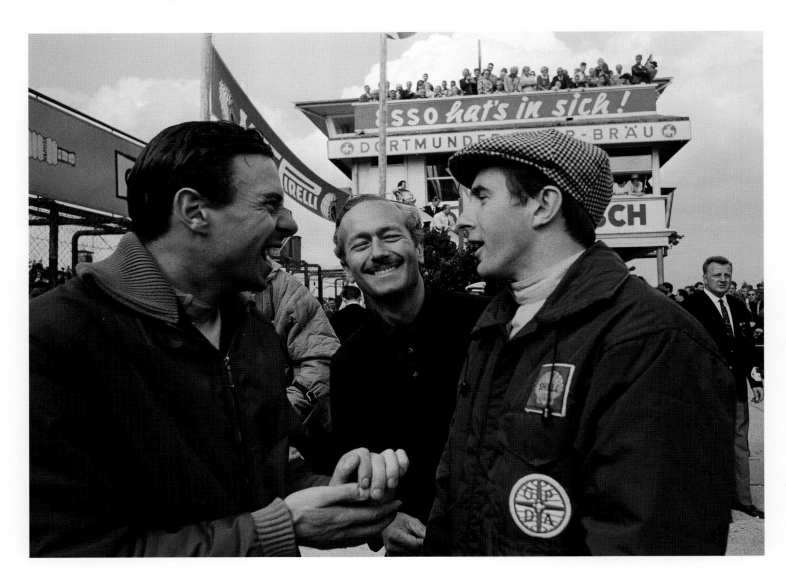

durchschnittlich zehn damals) dampft die innere Zuwendung ein, die wir ihnen schenken. Beim GP von Europa 2010 hob der Red Bull von Mark Webber mit fast 300 km/h in Richtung auf den blauen Himmel über Valencia ab, vollführte eine Riesen-Rolle und schlug anschließend mit immer noch hohem Tempo in die Streckenbegrenzung ein. Der Australier schüttelte sich und pfefferte wütend sein Hightech-Lenkrad aus dem Torso seines Wagens. Das war im Prinzip alles. Seit Ayrton Sennas Tod am 1. Mai 1994 herrscht eine neue Leichtigkeit. Wir haben das mögliche Ableben eines Formel-1-Fahrers in Ausübung seines Amtes aus unserem Bewusstsein getilgt. Die Dinge scheinen abzulaufen wie in einem Videospiel.

Webbers schnellen Vorgängern vor einem halben Jahrhundert hingegen wäre es dreckig ergangen. Sowie die Startflagge gefallen war, lauerte Gefahr. Nicht selten kündete ein schwarzer Rauchpilz am Horizont von einer Tragödie. Minuten dehnten sich zur Ewigkeit. Am 23. April 1962 musterte der Sport einen seiner Größten auf brutale Weise aus, als der Lotus von Stirling Moss auf dem Hochgeschwindigkeitskurs von Goodwood an einem Erdwall zerschellte. Dem kahlköpfigen Lenkrad-Akrobaten war künftig ein unruhig gelebter Ruhestand beschieden. „A Nodding Acquaintance with Death" titelte er später eines seiner Bücher über sich selbst – das Schwätzchen mit dem Tod über den Gartenzaun. Die Begegnung mit dem Sensenmann war ihnen allen geläufig, schon allein, weil sie immer wieder zu Augenzeugen des Sterbens der anderen wurden. Fast jedes Jahr krallte sich der Renntod ein bis zwei Opfer aus dem Fähnlein der 20 Verwegenen, die diesen Sport in seiner höchsten Erscheinungsform ausübten.

Kein Wunder: Da waren die Strecken, absurd gefährliche Naturkurse wie Spa-Francorchamps und der Nürburgring alter Art, 1921 beziehungsweise 1927 aus dem finsteren Tann von Ardennen und Eifel gehauen. Die Hecken, welche die „Grüne Hölle" bis 1970 säumten, boten so viel Schutz wie eine dichte Wolkendecke bei einem Flugzeugabsturz. Oder Monaco: Bis in der zweiten Hälfte der Sechziger die ersten Leitplanken aus dem Asphalt sprossen, drohten Bordsteine, Fassaden, Laternen und Balustraden die rasche Fahrt jäh zu stoppen. Eine schauerliche Ironie bestand darin, dass der tödliche Feuerunfall von Lorenzo Bandini 1967 auf erste, unbeholfene Sicherheitsvorkehrungen zurückzuführen war: Die Strohballen ausgangs der Hafen-Schikane waren mit Balken bewehrt, die den Ferrari in einen seitlichen Überschlag boxten.

Da waren die Wagen, fragile Geschöpfe, konstruiert für die normalen Belastungen eines Grand Prix und für sonst nichts. Manchmal waren sie selbst den Anforderungen nicht gewachsen, die ihr „Berufsleben" an sie stellte: „Immer, wenn mich ein Rad meines eigenen Autos überholt, weiß ich, dass ich in einem Lotus sitze", stänkerte Graham Hill gerne, ein Fall unter etlichen. Der Begriff Sicherheit gehörte lange Zeit nicht einmal zum Grundwortschatz des Grand-Prix-Piloten. Im Gegenteil – die Romantik seines Gewerbes leitete sich nicht zuletzt aus seiner Nähe zum Tod ab. Gegen Ende des Jahrzehnts begannen sich Männer wie Jackie Stewart energisch um mehr Sicherheit am rasenden Arbeitsplatz zu kümmern. Dass man sich etwa mit immer wirksamerer flammfester Wäsche verhüllte und mit Vollintegralhelmen behütete, zog ausgerechnet Hohn und Spott des unfallgeschädigten Puristen Stirling Moss auf sich. Da wachse, ließ er sich vernehmen, eine neue Spezies von Weicheiern und Warmduschern heran, die in diesem Sport eigentlich nichts zu suchen hätten. Und einer von den jungen Wilden applaudierte: Jacky Ickx.

Man fuhr gleichwohl gegen geringes Entgelt, aus Freude am Fahren. Die Generation der Sechziger war schier unermüdlich, fast an jedem Wochenende unterwegs, im Winter gern auch an exotischeren Schauplätzen wie im Rahmen der Tasman-Serie. Und sie glänzte durch Vielseitigkeit – im Gegensatz zu den Monokulturen, die heute bestellt werden. Nur ein paar Beispiele: Jim Clark, Formel-1-Weltmeister von 1963 und 1965, siegte 1965 auch in Indianapolis und war etwa im Lotus Cortina ein Tourenwagen-Pilot von hohem Unterhaltungswert. Graham Hill fügte seinen beiden Championaten von 1962 und 1968 Erfolge in Indy (1966) und in Le Mans (1972) an. Jochen Rindt, Grand-Prix-Titelträger 1970, holte sich den Sieg auf dem Sarthe-Kurs 1965. Sie nannten ihn den „König der Formel 2" – und in der Tat waren Ausritte in deren flinken kleinen Monoposti für einen Formel-1-Piloten Ehrensache und angenehme Verpflichtung. Jacky Ickx, Jo Siffert oder Pedro Rodriguez erwiesen sich als gleichermaßen begnadet im Grand-Prix-Fahrzeug wie im Sportwagen über die lange Distanz. Mit Mario Andretti schließlich ging aus der Dekade einer der größten Allrounder im Motorsport überhaupt hervor.

Die ständige Präsenz des ultimativen Risikos schweißte die Protagonisten jener Zeit viel mehr zusammen, als dies bei ihren Nachfahren anno 2010 in ihren diamantharten Kokons aus Kohlefaser der Fall ist. In seiner ebenso witzigen wie bewegenden Autobiographie „All Arms and Elbows" stellt Innes Ireland, selber stets zu Scherzen aufgelegt, die lebendige Kameraderie seiner Zeitgenossen heraus. Wo der aktuelle Formel-1-Set den Schauplatz seines letzten Einsatzes eilends verlässt wie den einer Amtshandlung, grundsätzlich getrennt reist und die Rivalen der Rennbahn einander argwöhnisch beäugen, wusste man zu feiern und schlug auch schon einmal über die Stränge, wie in der Promille-Seligkeit live zu besichtigen, in der in John Frankenheimers berühmtem Film-Epos „Grand Prix" von 1966 Siege zelebriert wurden. Bevor totale Kommerzialisierung und Verwissenschaftlichung diesen Sport erkalten ließen, kam der Frau vor Ort eine tragende Rolle zu, nicht nur als Zierde von Box und Fahrerlager, sondern indem sie Zeiten nahm, Runden-Zähltabellen führte und sich um Seele und Herz des Mannes an ihrer Seite verdient machte.

Natürlich war auch der Rennsport der sechziger Jahre in Vergangenheit und Zukunft eingebettet. Mit der 2,5-Liter-Formel – letztes Jahr 1960 – ragte eine Epoche in sie hinein, deren automobile Zeugnisse sich nach (Frontmotor-) Architektur und Erscheinungsbild an die Boliden der Dreißiger anlehnten, Ausnahme: die Silberpfeile, welche die Auto Union damals in die deutsch-deutsche Schlacht geschickt hatte. Die wurden von einem Spötter mal so definiert: vier Meter Motortrakt, ein Notsitz vorn. Durch die Dreiliter-Ära, die 1966 eher zögerlich begann und bis 1986 andauerte, waren die Sechziger mit künftigen Dekaden vernetzt. Einen Meilenstein grub gleichwohl Jim Clarks Sieg in Zandvoort 1967 ein, in einem Lotus 49, im Nacken des Piloten der just geschaffene kompakte Ford-Achtzylinder namens DFV (für *double four valve* wegen seiner beiden Bänke und jeweils vier Ventilen je Zylinder). Er prägte die Formel 1 fast 20 Jahre, letzter Triumph: durch Michele Alboreto in einem Tyrrell 1983 in Detroit.

Herzstück und komplett Eigentum und Eigentümlichkeit der Sechziger war die Formel 1 für Rennwagen bis 1,5 Liter zwischen 1961 und 1965. Diese Phase begann mit einer totalen Ferrari-Dominanz, führte über den praktisch in letzter Sekunde errungenen Titelgewinn für John Surtees in einem Wagen mit dem *cavallino rampante* und die rote Marke selbst bei den Konstrukteuren 1964 und mündete in einen Honda-Sieg beim letzten Rennen in Mexico City. Dennoch zementierte sie den Wachwechsel von den Italienern in den Fünfzigern (kurz unterbrochen durch die Jahre der Mercedes-Hegemonie 1954 und 1955) zu den Briten. Ferner zeichnete sie sich aus durch eine erstaunliche Artenvielfalt und geradezu demokratische Breite hinsichtlich der Anzahl der Teilnehmer: In ihren fünf Jahren Verweildauer und 46 Großen Preisen waren 101 Piloten in den Fahrzeugen von 21 Marken unterwegs.

An der Spitze indessen machten die üblichen Verdächtigen in den üblichen Fabrikaten die Dinge untereinander aus, wenn nicht gerade ein Glücksfall eintrat wie der Sieg des Grand-Prix-Novizen Giancarlo Baghetti beim GP de France 1961 in Reims. Als der überragende Fahrer der Epoche galt Jim Clark. Aber es gab genügend Männer, die dem Schotten zumindest schwer zu schaffen machen konnten. Immerhin brachten die sechziger Jahre sieben Weltmeister hervor. Da war der Australier Jack Brabham, wortkarg-entschlossen und ein unerbittlicher Gegner auf der Piste. Von ihm stammt der viel zitierte Satz: „When the flag drops, the bullshit stops." So richtig traute er nur sich selbst, baute ab 1962 seine eigenen Autos, gewann 1966 in Reims als Erster einen Grand Prix in einem Fahrzeug, das seinen eigenen Namen trug.

Da war Phil Hill, der sich 1961 mit nur zwei Saison-Siegen als erster Amerikaner in die Liste der Meister eintrug, ein Gentleman und Feingeist, der einmal zu spät zum Training erschien, weil er eine Messe von Mozart im Autoradio zu Ende gehört hatte. Da war sein Namensvetter Graham, der schnauzbärtige Londoner. Der englische Hill verschliss nach seiner zweiten Weltmeisterschaft seinen Ruhm und sein Renommee, weil er einfach nicht aufhören konnte mit diesem Sport. 1975 tat er es dann doch und verunglückte im November des Jahres tödlich mit dem Flugzeug. Das hört sich an wie Hohn. Da war Jim Clark selber, den viele noch heute für den größten Rennfahrer aller Zeiten halten, obwohl ihm zäh das Klischee anhaftete, er sei ein simpler schottischer Schafhirte, der sich auf den Renn-Parcours verirrt hatte.

Da war John Surtees, Umsteiger vom Rennmotorrad, „der einzige Champion auf zwei und auf vier Rädern", wie dem Publikum in stereotyper Wiederholung eingehämmert wurde. Da war der Neuseeländer Denis Hulme, genannt „der Bär", der sich durch stoische Gelassenheit und urige Verlässlichkeit auszeichnete. Und da war Jackie Stewart, der „fliegende Schotte" Nummer zwei in chronologischer Reihenfolge. Bereits durch Platz sechs bei seinem ersten Grand Prix im Januar 1965 im südafrikanischen East London, Position drei beim GP de Monaco fünf Monate später und den Sieg in Monza im selben Jahr empfahl er sich für höhere Weihen, die ihm als Dreifach-Champion 1969, 1971 und 1973 dann auch reichlich zuteilwurden. Jede Auswahl unter den restlichen ist subjektiv. Auch sie – wie manche andere – prägten die sechziger Jahre in der Formel 1: der notorische Pechvogel Chris Amon, der lange Amerikaner Dan Gurney, der ausschaute wie ein Wikinger, der sich im Jahrhundert vertan hatte, der verwegene Belgier Jacky Ickx, Bruce McLaren, Neuseeländer wie Amon und gleichermaßen versiert als Pilot wie als Konstrukteur von Rennwagen, der aufstrebende Jochen Rindt.

Enzo Ferrari betrachtete und verachtete seinen englischen Widersacher Colin Chapman, Firmengründer, Chef und Einsatzleiter bei Lotus, als „Garagisten" – als einen, der aus Serienteilen und ein paar eigenen Zutaten Rennautos zusammenschustert. Dennoch liefen bereits die sechziger Jahre auf ein Duell zwischen diesen beiden Exponenten sehr unterschiedlicher Philosophien hinaus – entschieden bewahrender Denkungsart der eine, ultraprogressiv der andere. Chapmans Kreationen wie der Lotus 25 von 1962 mit seinem Monocoque-Rückgrat revolutionierten die schnelle Zunft ebenso wie der einträgliche Geistesblitz, seinen hurtigen Fuhrpark ab 1968 in den bunten Farben des branchenfernen Sponsors Gold Leaf zu lackieren.

1970 geriet in vielerlei Hinsicht zur Gelenkstelle in der Grand-Prix-Geschichte, fast schon zum Kontrapunkt zu den zehn Jahren davor. Die Formel 1 verlor Bruce McLaren, Piers Courage und Jochen Rindt an den Tod und Jack Brabham und Dan Gurney an den Ruhestand, gewann hingegen junge Talente wie Clay Regazzoni, Emerson Fittipaldi, Ronnie Peterson und François Cevert.

Die Faszination blieb. Aber das Ambiente hatte sich geändert.

La Formule 1 dans les années soixante
Un exercise de style

Le temps est une variable. À la demande de journalistes, Albert Einstein fut à l'époque prié de nous expliquer, de manière compréhensible, sa théorie de la relativité. Le génie espiègle répondit alors d'un ton narquois : « Imaginez-vous, assis cinq minutes sur un canapé à côté d'une jolie fille ou les fesses à l'air sur un poêle chauffé à blanc. Vous comprendrez alors le fond de ma pensée. » Les années vingt ont été différemment ressenties, vécues et perçues que les années cinquante. Suivre un Grand Prix en direct laisse plus de traces dans notre façon de percevoir le temps que de lire assidûment la presse locale après le petit-déjeuner.

Mais même dans ce cas, une petite différenciation s'impose. Un Grand Prix dans la première décennie du troisième millénaire sollicite nettement moins la perception comme elle aurait pu l'être au cours d'une compétition dans les années soixante. Rien que le simple nombre de courses automobiles organisées par saison de nos jours (19 en 2010 contre en moyenne dix à l'époque) estompe, avec l'habitude, l'attachement que nous leur avons porté. Lors du GP d'Europe 2010, la Red Bull de Mark Webber lancée à près de 300 km/h effectue un vol plané en direction du ciel bleu au-dessus de Valence, effectue un looping spectaculaire avant de terminer sa course à pleine vitesse dans le mur de pneus. L'Australien s'ébroue et balance enragé le volant high-tech hors du cockpit de sa voiture. Rien de plus à ajouter. Depuis la disparition tragique d'Ayrton Senna le 1er mai 1994, une nouvelle forme d'insouciance règne. Nous avons effacé de notre conscience la possibilité qu'un pilote de Formule 1 puisse périr dans l'exercice de ses fonctions. Les choses semblent se dérouler comme dans un jeu vidéo.

Il y a un demi-siècle de cela, les prédécesseurs de Webber ne s'en seraient, par contre, pas sortis indemnes. Aussitôt le départ donné, le danger guettait. Un champignon de fumée noire à l'horizon laissait bien souvent présager une tragédie. Les minutes devenaient éternité. Le 23 avril 1962, la discipline reine écarte brutalement l'un de ses plus grands champions, lorsque la Lotus de Stirling Moss s'écrase contre un talus sur le circuit de Goodwood. Le chauve, un as du volant, semble alors destiné à une retraite loin d'être de tout repos. Par la suite, il intitulera l'un de ses livres autobiographiques « A Nodding Acquaintance with Death », un entretien à bâtons rompus avec la Mort. Chacun d'eux avait déjà côtoyé la « Grande Faucheuse », ne serait-ce que parce qu'ils avaient assisté plus d'une fois impuissants au décès brutal d'autres coureurs. Rares étaient les années sans que la mort ne jette son dévolu sur l'un ou l'autre de la chevauchée des 20 téméraires après avoir porté ce sport à son maximum.

Rien de surprenant : les circuits, des pistes en milieu naturel extrêmement dangereux, comme le Spa-Francorchamps et l'ancien tracé du Nürburgring, ont été taillés en 1921 pour l'un et en 1927 pour l'autre à travers les forêts obscures des Ardennes et d'Eifel. Les haies, bordant le « Grüne Hölle » (l'Enfer vert) jusqu'en 1970, offraient autant de protection à un coureur qu'une épaisse couverture nuageuse à un avion avant son crash. Ou encore le circuit urbain de Monaco : jusqu'à ce que les premières glissières de sécurité jaillissent du bitume dans la seconde moitié des années soixante, bordures de trottoir, façades, lanternes et balustrades menaçaient de mettre soudainement fin aux courses folles. Ironie effroyable de l'histoire : l'accident mortel en 1967 de Lorenzo Bandini pris au piège sous sa voiture en feu s'explique notamment par les premières mesures de sécurité trop maladroites. Les bottes de paille à la sortie de la chicane du port étaient armées de barres qui propulsèrent la Ferrari sur le côté, avant qu'elle ne parte en tonneaux et se retourne sur le pilote.

Les voitures, de fragiles créatures, étaient conçues pour résister aux conditions normales d'un Grand Prix et à rien d'autre. Les bolides n'étaient parfois même pas à la hauteur des exigences techniques rudimentaires : « chaque fois qu'une roue de ma propre voiture me doublait, je savais que j'étais au volant d'une Lotus », souligne Graham Hill en râlant, un exemple parmi tant d'autres. Le terme *sécurité* ne faisait même pas partie du vocabulaire de base d'un pilote de Grand Prix. Bien au contraire, la vision romantique de ce métier était étroitement liée à la proximité avec la mort. Vers la fin de la décennie, de grands noms tels que Jackie Stewart commencent à s'engager pour une sécurité accrue en course automobile. Le fait de porter par exemple des sous-vêtements ignifugés de plus en plus résistants et un casque intégral suscita paradoxalement quelques sarcasmes de la part du puriste Stirling Moss qui avait pourtant payé le prix fort. Selon lui, une nouvelle espèce de figues molles et de poules mouillées, qui n'avait absolument pas sa place dans ce sport, était en train de se développer. Des propos qui enchantèrent l'un des jeunes loups aux dents longues : Jacky Ickx.

    Les rémunérations étaient loin d'être mirobolantes, seule la passion comptait. La génération des années soixante était pour ainsi dire increvable, presque tous les week-ends en compétition, en hiver de préférence sous des cieux plus exotiques comme celui de la Formule Tasmane. Et les pilotes de cette époque brillaient par leur polyvalence, à l'inverse des « monocultures » cultivées dans la société d'aujourd'hui. Quelques exemples suffisent : Jim Clark, double champion du monde de Formule 1 en 1963 et 1965, inscrit la même année les 500 miles d'Indianapolis à son palmarès et se montre très éclectique en participant à des courses de voitures de tourisme à bord de la Lotus Cortina. Graham Hill réalise un triplé inoubliable : champion de F1 en 1962 et en 1968, il s'impose au Indy 500 (1966) et remporte les 24 heures du Mans (1972). Jochen Rindt, sacré champion du monde au Grand Prix en 1970, décroche la victoire sur le circuit de la Sarthe en 1965. On lui donna le surnom de « Roi de la Formule 2 » : les sorties à bord de ces petits monoplaces rapides étaient aux yeux du pilote de F1 une affaire d'honneur et une obligation divertissante. Jacky Ickx, Jo Siffert ou encore Pedro Rodriguez se sont avérés être des pilotes d'exception tant au volant d'un bolide lors d'un Grand Prix que dans une voiture de sport sur de longues distances. Sans oublier Mario Andretti, incontestablement l'un des plus grands multi-talents du sport automobile de cette décennie.
    La présence constante du risque ultime soudait bien plus les protagonistes de cette époque que leurs descendants ne peuvent l'être en 2010, installés dans leurs cocons en fibres de carbone et durs comme du béton.

Dans son autobiographie à la fois drôle et émouvante « All Arms and Elbows », Innes Ireland, ayant lui-même toujours le mot pour rire, met en avant la profonde camaraderie qui unissait ses semblables. Là où de nos jours le cortège s'empresse de quitter la scène de sa dernière représentation une fois sa mission remplie, où ses membres voyagent par principe séparément et où les adversaires s'épient du coin de l'œil, on savait autrefois faire la fête et même pousser le bouchon un peu trop loin. Il suffit de s'en convaincre en regardant le célèbre « Grand Prix », superproduction de John Frankenheimer en 1966, et la manière dont on célébrait la victoire dans un état de félicité éthylique avancée. Avant que la commercialisation totale et la « scientifisation » ne viennent émousser la ferveur, la femme jouait un rôle fondamental sur un circuit : d'une part, sa beauté illuminait le stand et le parc des coureurs, et d'autre part, elle chronométrait les temps de passages, elle notait les tours sur les panneaux d'affichage et était aux petits soins pour l'homme à ses côtés.

Le sport automobile des années soixante s'inscrivait bien entendu dans la continuité des décennies précédentes tout en ayant une longueur d'avance. La cylindrée de 2,5 litres autorisée jusqu'en 1960 était la dernière d'une époque révolue, les modèles s'inspiraient des bolides des années trente en matière d'architecture (moteur à l'avant) et de design, à une exception près : les « flèches d'argent » de l'Auto Union. Les railleries allaient bon train : un engin motorisé sur quatre mètres et un strapontin à l'avant. La Formule 1 change d'ère avec le passage au moteur trois litres qui s'impose assez tardivement en 1966 et durera jusqu'en 1986, permettant ainsi aux années soixante de faire le lien avec les décennies à venir. La victoire de Jim Clark à Zandvoort en 1967 restera toutefois gravée dans les mémoires : le pilote au volant d'une Lotus 49, serré de près par le tout dernier moteur compact huit cylindres de Ford baptisé DFV (pour *double four valve* en raison de ses doubles arbres à cames et quatre soupapes par cylindre). Il marquera l'histoire de la Formule 1 pendant près de 20 ans. Michele Alboreto et l'écurie Tyrrell lui donneront sa dernière victoire dans les rues de Détroit en 1983.

Entre 1961 et 1965, la Formule 1 est dans les mains exclusives des moteurs de 1,5 litres maximum, pièces maîtresses et ainsi particularité des années soixante. Ce nouveau cycle débute par une nette domination Ferrari, en

passant par un triomphe sans partage avec le titre pilote décroché in extremis par John Surtees au volant d'une voiture arborant le mythique *cavallino rampante* (cheval cabré) et le titre constructeur enlevé par la marque rouge en 1964, et se termine avec la victoire de Honda lors de la dernière course à Mexico City. Les années cinquante dominées par les Italiens (avec un bref intermezzo de Mercedes en 1954 et 1955), les Britanniques reprennent néanmoins le flambeau et confortent leur position. Par ailleurs, cette ère se distingue par une étonnante diversité des genres et un large éventail quasi démocratique des participants : en cinq années de présence et sur 46 Grands Prix, on compte 101 pilotes pour 21 écuries.

En pole position toutefois, on retrouve toujours les mêmes, au volant des modèles habituels, réglant leurs petites affaires entre eux, excepté ce coup de chance quand le coureur novice, Giancarlo Baghetti, remporte la victoire au GP de France en 1961 à Reims. Jim Clark était à l'époque la référence dans le sport automobile. Sans pour autant sous-estimer certains pilotes qui pouvaient encore donner du fil à retordre à la légende écossaise. N'oublions pas que les années soixante ont vu naître sept champions du monde. Parmi lesquels l'Australien Jack Brabham, un personnage taciturne mais déterminé et un adversaire impitoyable sur le circuit, qui lança cette phrase mémorable : « When the flag drops, the bullshit stops ». Il n'avait confiance qu'en lui-même, se met à construire ses propres voitures à partir de 1962, est le premier à remporter un Grand Prix (Reims, 1966) au volant d'une voiture portant son nom.

Et Phil Hill, premier coureur américain à s'inscrire en 1961 sur la liste des champions avec seulement deux victoires en une saison. Un gentleman et un esprit de finesse qui manqua même le début de son entraînement pour écouter une messe de Mozart dans son intégralité sur son autoradio. Et son homonyme Graham, le Londonien à moustache. Après son deuxième championnat du monde, la gloire et la renommée du Britannique commencent à se ternir, ne pouvant tirer un trait sur ce sport. En 1975, il quittera finalement le cockpit, avant de trouver la mort la même année dans un accident d'avion. Un dernier pied de nez du destin. Et Jim Clark en personne, que beaucoup considère encore aujourd'hui comme le plus grand pilote de tous les temps, bien qu'il soit difficilement indissociable du cliché de simple berger écossais qui se serait égaré sur le circuit.

Sans oublier John Surtees, ancien pilote motocycliste, « le seul champion à avoir cumulé les titres mondiaux sur deux et quatre roues », comme se plaisaient à le répéter les médias. Et le Néo-Zélandais Denis Hulme, surnommé « l'ours » et caractérisé par un sang-froid stoïque et une fiabilité démodée. Et Jackie Stewart, l'« Ecossais volant », classé numéro deux dans l'ordre chronologique. Pour sa première participation à une course, le Grand Prix d'Afrique du Sud sur le circuit d'East London en janvier 1965, il termine sixième, cinq mois plus tard il décrochera la troisième place lors du GP de Monaco et la même année le titre de champion sur le circuit de Monza. Un parcours qui le prédestinait à la consécration suprême qui lui sera dévolue en décrochant le titre de triple champion du monde en 1969, 1971 et 1973. Faire un choix parmi les autres serait subjectif. Qui dit Formule 1 des années soixante, dit aussi bien d'autres grandes pointures : Chris Amon considéré comme le pilote de talent le plus malchanceux, l'Américain de grande taille Dan Gurney à l'allure de Viking qui semblait s'être trompé de siècle, Jacky Ickx le casse-cou belge, Bruce McLaren d'origine néo-zélandaise comme Amon et à la carrière de pilote et de constructeur bien remplie, l'étoile montante Jochen Rindt.

Enzo Ferrari méprisait et qualifiait son adversaire anglais Colin Chapman, à la fois père fondateur, chef d'écurie et ingénieur chez Lotus, de « garagiste », seulement capable de bricoler des voitures de course à partir de pièces de série et de quelques produits faits maison. Mais les années soixante annonçaient déjà le duel entre ces deux principaux protagonistes imprégnés de philosophies très différentes, l'un à la mentalité résolument conservatrice, l'autre ultra-progressive. Les créations de Chapman, telles que la Lotus 25 (1962) à châssis monocoque, révolutionnent à l'époque le monde de la course extrême, tout comme son trait de génie, à savoir mettre dès 1968 ses bolides aux couleurs vives du sponsor Gold Leaf, n'ayant certes rien à voir avec le sport automobile.

L'année 1970 fait figure de pièce angulaire à bien des points de vue dans l'histoire des Grands Prix, voire de contrepoint par rapport aux dix années précédentes. La Formule 1 déplore la perte tragique de Bruce McLaren, Piers Courage et Jochen Rindt, tandis que Jack Brabham et Dan Gurney prennent leur retraite. La relève était cependant assurée par de jeunes talents comme Clay Regazzoni, Emerson Fittipaldi, Ronnie Peterson et François Cevert.

La fascination se perpétue. Mais l'ambiance n'est plus la même.

La Formula 1 en los años sesenta

Retrato del espíritu de la epoca

El tiempo es una variable. En una ocasión, algunos periodistas pidieron a Albert Einstein que explicara su teoría de la relatividad de forma gráfica. "Imaginen", comenzó el pícaro genio, "que pasan cinco minutos sentados en el sofá junto a una mujer hermosa, o con el trasero sobre la placa de la cocina al rojo vivo. Entonces comprenderán lo que quiero decir". Los años veinte se experimentaron, vivieron y sintieron de forma distinta a los cincuenta. En nuestra sensación del tiempo, un Gran Premio se hace notar de forma mucho más enérgica que leyendo la extensa crónica del diario local tras el desayuno.

Sin embargo, incluso aquí hay diferencias. Un Gran Premio en la primera década del tercer milenio fuerza nuestra percepción con menor intensidad de lo que habría sido el caso en los años sesenta. El simple número de pruebas que conforman el ciclo anual en nuestra época (en 2010 son 19, frente a una media de 10 en aquel entonces) atenúa la atención interior que les ofrecemos. En el GP de Europa de 2010, el Red Bull de Mark Webber despegó en dirección al cielo azul sobre Valencia a casi 300 km/h, completó una enorme voltereta para estrellarse a continuación, aún a gran velocidad, contra las protecciones de la pista. El australiano se sacudió y, furioso, arrojó

el modernísimo volante fuera del torso de su choche. Eso fue todo. Desde la muerte de Ayrton Senna el 1 de mayo de 1994 se respira un ambiente mucho más relajado. Hemos borrado de nuestra conciencia la posible defunción de un piloto de Fórmula 1 en el ejercicio de su trabajo. Todo parece transcurrir como en un videojuego.

Hace medio siglo, los veloces antecesores de Webber lo habrían tenido mucho más crudo. El peligro acechaba desde que caía la bandera de salida. A menudo, una columna de humo negro en el horizonte anunciaba una tragedia. Los minutos se hacían eternos. El 23 de abril de 1962, el deporte eliminaba a uno de los más grandes de forma brutal, cuando el Lotus de Stirling Moss se estrellaba en un terraplén del circuito de alta velocidad de Goodwood. Para el acróbata del volante de cabeza pelada, el comienzo de una agitada jubilación. "A Nodding Acquaintance with Death" tituló tiempo después uno de sus libros sobre sí mismo –la breve charla con la muerte. El encuentro con el hombre de la guadaña era algo corriente para todos ellos, por el simple hecho de que eran continuamente testigos de la muerte de los demás. Casi todos los años, las carreras se cobraban la vida de una o dos víctimas de la parrilla de 20 osados que practicaban este deporte en su forma más elevada.

Ninguna sorpresa: Estaban los circuitos, trazados absurdamente peligrosos como Spa-Francorchamps y Nürburgring en sus versiones antiguas, esculpidos en los oscuros bosques de coníferas de las regiones de Ardenas y Eifel, en 1921 y 1927 respectivamente. Los setos que flanqueaban el "infierno verde" hasta 1970 ofrecían la misma protección que un manto de nubes durante un accidente aéreo. O Mónaco: hasta que los primeros guardarraíles brotaron del asfalto en la segunda mitad de los sesenta, bordillos, fachadas y farolas amenazaban con poner fin a la carrera de forma dramática. La estremecedora ironía es que el fuego que costó la vida a Lorenzo Bandini en 1967 se debió a las torpes medidas de seguridad iniciales: Las balas de paja en la salida de la chicane del puerto estaban asentadas sobre postes, los cuales hicieron volcar al Ferrari.

También hay que mencionar los coches, frágiles criaturas, construidas para soportar los esfuerzos normales de un Gran Premio y nada más. A veces, ni siquiera estaban a la altura de las exigencias de su "vida laboral": "Cada vez que me adelanta una rueda de mi propio coche, se que voy en un Lotus", solía criticar Graham Hill con indisimulada ironía, por citar alguno de los casos. Durante mucho tiempo, el término seguridad ni siquiera aparecía en el vocabulario básico de los pilotos de Gran Premio. Al contrario –el romanticismo de su empresa se basaba, en gran medida, en la cercanía de la muerte. A finales de la década, hombres como Jackie Stewart comenzaron a preocuparse seriamente por la seguridad en sus vertiginosos puestos de trabajo. Cubrirse con prendas ignífugas cada vez más resistentes y protegerse con cascos integrales, provocó las burlas precisamente del accidentado purista Stirling Moss. Está surgiendo, declaró, una nueva especie de lloricas y blandengues, a la que no se le ha perdido nada en este deporte. Uno de los impetuosos jóvenes aplaudía: Jacky Ickx.

La recompensa también era menor, se corría por puro placer. La generación de los sesenta era prácticamente incansable, en movimiento casi todos los fines de semana, citándose con gusto en invierno en lugares exóticos, como en el marco de las Tasman Series. Además, brillaba por su universalidad, al contrario de los monocultivos encargados hoy en día. Por poner sólo algunos ejemplos: Jim Clark, campeón del mundo de Fórmula 1 en 1963 y 1965, ganó también en Indianápolis en 1965 y, en su Lotus Cortina, daba espectáculo como piloto de turismos. Graham Hill añadió a sus dos campeonatos de 1962 y 1968 éxitos en Indy (1966) y Le Mans (1972). Jochen Rindt, dueño del título de Grandes Premios de 1970, se hizo con la victoria en el circuito de la Sarthe en 1965. Lo llamaban el "Rey de la F2" –y efectivamente, las excursiones en los pequeños y ágiles monoplazas eran una cuestión de honor y una agradable obligación para cualquier piloto de Fórmula 1. Jacky Ickx, Jo Siffert o Pedro Rodríguez mostraron su talento tanto en los coches de Gran Premio, como en los coches deportivos en pruebas de resistencia. Por último, la década alumbró a Mario Andretti, uno de los talentos del deporte del motor más completos de la historia.

La constante presencia del mayor de los riesgos tejía entre los protagonistas de aquella época lazos de unión mucho más fuertes que los de sus sucesores de 2010, en sus durísimos capullos de fibra de carbono. En su tan divertida como emotiva autobiografía "All Arms and Elbows", Innes Ireland, siempre dispuesto para bromear, destacaba la gran camaradería de sus coetáneos. Donde el set actual de la Fórmula 1 abandona a toda prisa el lugar de su última actuación, como si de un acto oficial se tratara, viajando generalmente por separado, y donde los rivales de la pista se observan unos a otros con recelo, en aquellos tiempos se sabía festejar y, de vez en cuando, los protagonistas se pasaban de rosca, como mostraba la hermandad etílica en la que se celebraban las victorias, plasmada en el famoso clásico de John Frankenheimer "Grand Prix", de 1966. Antes de que la total comercialización y los avances tecnológicos enfriaran este deporte, las mujeres tenían asignado un papel fundamental, no sólo como ornamento en el box y en el paddock, sino tomando los tiempos de carrera, llevando las tablas de resultados y comprometiéndose con el alma y el corazón del hombre a su lado.

Por supuesto, las carreras de los sesenta también estaban incrustadas entre el pasado y el futuro. Con la Fórmula de 2,5 litros –disputada por última vez en 1960– comenzó una época cuyos testigos sobre ruedas se asemejaban en su arquitectura (motor delantero) y en su apariencia a los bólidos de los años treinta, con una excepción: las Flechas de Plata, enviadas a la batalla fratricida entre alemanes por Auto Union. Un detractor se burlaba de ellas definiéndolas de la siguiente manera: cuatro metros de motor, un asiento de emergencia delante. Con la era de los motores de 3 litros, que comenzó titubeante en 1966 y se prolongó hasta 1986, los sesenta estaban conectados con décadas futuras. La victoria de Jim Clark en Zandvoort 1967 también fue todo un hito, lograda en un Lotus 49, en el cogote del piloto el compacto motor de 8 cilindros de Ford llamado DFV (*double four valve*, por sus dos bancos y sus cuatro válvulas por cilindro). Marcó la Fórmula 1 durante casi 20 años, hasta su último triunfo: Michele Alboreto al volante de un Tyrrell, 1983 en Detroit.

Corazón y propiedad exclusiva y característica de los sesenta era la Fórmula 1 para coches hasta 1,5 litros entre 1961 y 1965. Esa fase comenzó con un dominio incontestable de Ferrari, continuó en 1964 con el título de John Surtees, logrado in extremis en un coche con el *cavallino rampante*, y el de la propia marca roja en el campeonato de constructores, para desembocar en una victoria de Honda en la última carrera en Ciudad de México. Sin embargo, esta fase puso los cimientos del cambio de guardia de los italianos (brevemente interrumpida por el dominio de Mercedes en 1954 y 1955) a los británicos. Por otro lado, se caracterizó por una impresionante variedad y una casi democrática amplitud en cuanto al número participantes: En sus cinco años de permanencia y sus 46 Grandes Premios participaron 101 pilotos en vehículos de 21 marcas.

Mientras tanto, los sospechosos habituales en las marcas habituales se disputaban las victorias, si es que no sucedía algo extraordinario, como la victoria del debutante Giancarlo Baghetti en el GP de Francia de 1961 en Reims. Jim Clark era considerado el mejor piloto de la época. Pero había bastantes hombres capaces de, cuando menos, poner en aprietos al escocés. Después de todo, los sesenta coronaron a siete campeones del mundo diferentes. Estaba el australiano Jack Brabham, decidido, de pocas palabras y un implacable rival en la pista. Suya es la conocida frase: "When the flag drops, the bullshit stops". Sólo se fiaba de sí mismo, desde 1962 construía sus propios coches, en Reims 1966 se convirtió en el primero en ganar un Gran Premio en un vehículo con su nombre.

Allí estaba Phil Hill, el cual se convirtió en 1961, con sólo dos victorias, en el primer americano en incluir su nombre en la lista de campeones, caballero y cultivado, capaz de llegar tarde a un entrenamiento porque había escuchado hasta el final una misa de Mozart en la radio de su coche. Allí estaba su tocayo Graham, el bigotudo londinense. El Hill inglés gastó tras su segundo título mundial su gloria y su fama, simplemente porque no podía dejar este deporte. En 1975 lo hizo por fin, muriendo en noviembre del mismo año en accidente aéreo. Suena como una burla del destino. Allí estaba el propio Jim Clark, considerado aún hoy por muchos como el mejor piloto de todos los tiempos, a pesar de que no conseguía sacudirse el cliché de ser un simple pastor escocés, que se había extraviado en el circuito.

Allí estaba John Surtees, venido del motociclismo, "el único campeón sobre dos y cuatro ruedas", estereotipo con el que se machacaba al público una y otra vez. Allí estaba el neozelandés Denis Hulme, apodado "el oso", el cual destacaba por su estoica serenidad y su castiza fiabilidad. Y allí estaba Jackie Stewart, el "escocés volador", segundo en orden cronológico. Con el sexto puesto en el primer Gran Premio en enero de 1965 en East London, Sudáfrica, el tercer puesto en el Gran Premio de Mónaco cinco meses después y la victoria en Monza ese mismo año, se había postulado para la gloria, la cual obtuvo sobradamente con sus tres títulos en 1969, 1971 y 1973. Toda selección entre el resto es subjetiva. También ellos –como algunos más– marcaron los sesenta en la Fórmula 1: El muy desafortunado Chris Amon, el larguirucho americano Dan Gurney, con su aspecto de vikingo perdido en el siglo equivocado, el audaz belga Jacky Ickx, Bruce McLaren, neozelandés como Amon y tan versado pilotando como construyendo coches de carreras, el floreciente Jochen Rindt.

Enzo Ferrari consideraba y denominaba en tono despreciativo a su adversario inglés Colin Chapman, fundador, jefe y director de operaciones de Lotus, como "garajista" –alguien que improvisaba coches de carreras con piezas de serie y un par de ingredientes propios. A pesar de todo, ya en los sesenta se avecinaba un duelo entre estos dos exponentes de tan diferentes filosofías –uno de mentalidad decididamente conservacionista, el otro ultraprogresista. Las creaciones de Chapman, como el Lotus 25 de 1962, con su columna vertebral monocasco, revolucionaron el veloz gremio, tanto como la rentable idea de pintar a partir de 1968 su rápido parque móvil en los llamativos colores del patrocinador Gold Leaf, totalmente ajeno a las carreras.

En muchos aspectos, 1970 marcó un punto de inflexión en la historia de los Grandes Premios, casi como contrapunto de los diez años anteriores. La Fórmula 1 perdió a Bruce McLaren, Piers Courage y Jochen Rindt a manos de la muerte, mientras que Jack Brabham y Dan Gurney se retiraron, aunque ganó jóvenes talentos como Clay Regazzoni, Emerson Fittipaldi, Ronnie Peterson y François Cevert.

La fascinación se mantuvo. Pero el ambiente ya no era el mismo.

La Formula 1 negli anni sessanta
Spirito di un'epoca

Il tempo è una variabile. Un giorno ad Albert Einstein fu chiesto da alcuni giornalisti di spiegare in modo chiaro la teoria della relatività. "Immaginatevi" disse il genio beffardo "di trascorrere cinque minuti seduti su una poltrona assieme a una bella donna oppure su una piastra rovente. Allora capirete cosa intendo". Gli anni venti furono percepiti, vissuti e sentiti diversamente dagli anni cinquanta. Nella percezione del tempo, un Grand Prix risulta energicamente più marcato rispetto alla lettura approfondita del giornale locale dopo la colazione.

Ma anche qui va fatta una distinzione. Nel primo decennio del terzo millennio un Gran Premio richiama l'attenzione del pubblico con un'intensità di gran lunga minore rispetto a quanto sarebbe accaduto negli anni sessanta. Il nostro entusiasmo si affievolisce già solo per il numero di corse che ai nostri tempi si tengono nel ciclo di un anno (nel 2010 sono 19 contro una media di dieci di allora). Al GP europeo del 2010 la Red Bull di Mark Webber, a una velocità di quasi 300 km/h, ha preso il volo verso il cielo sopra Valencia, e dopo aver eseguito un loop di 360° ha infine terminato la sua corsa, sempre a velocità elevata, sbattendo contro le barriere di protezione. L'australiano, agitandosi, ha scaraventato, infuriato, il suo tecnologico volante dalla parte posteriore della vettura. Questo è quanto. Dopo la morte di Ayrton Senna avvenuta il 1 maggio 1994 regna una nuova leggerezza. Abbiamo cancellato dall'immaginario collettivo la possibile perdita di un pilota di Formula 1 nello svolgimento delle sue mansioni. Pare quasi di essere in un videogioco.

I veloci predecessori di Webber di mezzo secolo fa, invece, se la sarebbero vista male. Non appena abbassata la bandiera della partenza, il pericolo era imminente. Non di rado, un fungo nero di fumo all'orizzonte annunciava una tragedia. I minuti duravano un'eternità. Il 23 aprile 1962 il mondo sportivo perdeva in modo brutale uno dei suoi campioni, quando la Lotus di Stirling Moss si schiantò contro un terrapieno sulla pista veloce di Goodwood. In futuro, un periodo di ritiro vissuto in modo irrequieto attendeva il pelato acrobata del volante. "A Nodding Acquaintance with Death": così egli intitolò anni dopo una delle sue autobiografie, due chiacchiere con la morte oltre la siepe. L'incontro con la Morte era un'esperienza con la quale tutti avevano familiarità, già per il solo fatto di essere stati più e più volte testimoni della morte altrui. Quasi ogni anno la morte trascinava via con sé una o due vittime dal gruppo dei 20 temerari che praticavano questo sport nella sua forma di espressione più alta.

Il fatto non stupisce: un tempo, infatti, i tracciati – percorsi naturalistici assurdamente pericolosi come lo Spa-Francorchamps e il vecchio Nürburgring – erano stati ricavati, rispettivamente nel 1921 e nel 1927, dai cupi boschi delle Ardenne e dell'Eifel. Le boscaglie che fino al 1970 fiancheggiavano il circuito soprannominato l'"inferno verde" offrivano tanta protezione quanto una fitta coltre di nubi a un aereo in caduta. Oppure a Monaco: fino all'avvento dei primi guardrail, spuntati dall'asfalto verso la seconda metà degli anni sessanta, erano cordoli stradali, facciate, lampioni e balaustre a minacciare di arrestare bruscamente la rapida corsa. Per una tragica ironia della sorte, l'incidente in cui Lorenzo Bandini morì nel 1967 avvolto dalle fiamme fu da ricondursi proprio alle prime, maldestre misure di sicurezza: le balle di fieno poste all'uscita della chicane del porto erano rafforzate con pilastri, che trattennero la Ferrari capovolta su un fianco.

Le vetture di allora, fragili creature, erano realizzate per sopportare le normali sollecitazioni di un Grand Prix e null'altro. Talvolta non erano neppure idonee a soddisfare i requisiti loro posti dalla "professione": "Ogni volta che mi supera una ruota di una mia macchina, so di essere seduto in una Lotus", amava provocare Graham Hill, per citarne uno. Per lungo tempo il concetto di sicurezza non rientrava neppure nel vocabolario di base dei piloti del Gran Premio. Anzi, il romanticismo della professione era legato non da ultimo alla vicinanza alla morte. Verso la fine del decennio, uomini del calibro di Jackie Stewart incominciarono a battersi per una maggiore sicurezza sulla pista. Il fatto che ci si avvolgesse in tute ignifughe sempre più efficaci e ci si proteggesse con caschi integrali attirò lo scherno e il disprezzo del purista incidentato Stirling Moss: a suo parere stava nascendo una nuova generazione di pappamolle e senza fegato, che di fatto non avevano nulla da cercare in questo sport. E uno dei giovani selvaggi applaudiva: Jacky Ickx.

Eppure si correva per pochi soldi, per la mera gioia di guidare. La generazione degli anni sessanta era praticamente instancabile, in giro quasi ogni fine settimana, durante la stagione invernale anche in posti esotici, come nell'ambito della formula Tasman. E si distingueva per la sua versatilità in contrasto con le monoculture praticate al giorno d'oggi. Solo alcuni esempi: Jim Clark, campione del mondo di Formula 1 nel 1963 e 1965, nel 1965 vinse anche a Indianapolis e a bordo della Cortina Lotus fu un pilota di vetture Turismo di elevato valore intrattenitivo. Graham Hill, ai due campionati del 1962 e del 1968 aggiunse i successi di Indy (1966) e Le Mans (1972). Jochen Rindt, vincitore del Gran Premio del 1970, conquistò la vittoria anche sul percorso la Sarthe nel 1965. Lo chiamavano il "re della Formula 2", e di fatto per un pilota di Formula 1 le uscite sulle piccole e veloci monoposto erano una questione di onore e un piacevole obbligo. Jacky Ickx, Jo Siffert o Pedro Rodriguez dimostrarono tutti di essere dotati di grande talento sia nelle vetture Grand Prix sia in quelle sportive sulla lunga distanza. Infine, con Mario Andretti, emerse dalla decade uno dei maggiori talenti versatili dello sport automobilistico.

La persistente presenza del rischio di morte teneva legati i protagonisti di quell'epoca molto di più di quanto avvenga nei loro successori del 2010, avvolti nei loro bozzoli, duri come il diamante, in fibra al carbonio. Nella sua tanto divertente, quanto toccante autobiografia intitolata "All Arms and Elbows" Innes Ireland, racconta, sempre con un piglio ironico, del vivace cameratismo tra i suoi contemporanei. Mentre il set attuale di Formula 1 abbandona la scena dell'ultima competizione come fosse un atto d'ufficio, viaggia di norma separatamente e i rivali si scrutano con sospetto, allora si sapeva festeggiare e talora ci si lasciava andare, come nello stato di beatitudine etilica in cui venivano celebrate le vittorie nel famoso film-epopea "Grand Prix" girato da John Frankenheimer nel 1966. Prima che una totale commercializzazione e una scientificizzazione raffreddassero questo sport, le donne sul posto giocavano un ruolo fondamentale, non solo come splendida cornice ai box e alle manifestazioni, bensì tenendo i tempi, reggendo i tabelloni del numero di giri e apportando un prezioso supporto al cuore e all'anima dell'uomo al loro fianco.

Ovviamente, anche lo sport automobilistico degli anni sessanta era integrato nel passato e nel futuro. Con i motori a 2,5 litri – che corsero per l'ultima volta nel 1960 – iniziò una nuova epoca, le cui vetture si ispiravano per architettura (del motore frontale) e aspetto ai bolidi degli anni trenta, eccezione fatta per la "Freccia d'argento" che allora Auto Union aveva spedito nella battaglia tedesco-tedesca. Queste monoposto furono criticamente definite come "quattro metri di motore e un sedile di emergenza anteriore". Con l'era dei 3 litri, che incominciò con qualche esitazione nel 1966 per poi durare fino al 1986, gli anni sessanta erano indissolubilmente legati alle decadi successive. La vittoria di Jim Clark a Zandvoort nel 1967 segnò una pietra miliare, a bordo di una Lotus 49, alle spalle del pilota il compatto otto cilindri Ford di nuova creazione, denominato DFV (acronimo di *double four valve* per i suoi due monoblocchi e quattro valvole per cilindro). Esso segnò la Formula 1 per quasi 20 anni, con l'ultimo trionfo di Michele Alboreto in una Tyrrell nel 1983.

Il punto nevralgico degli anni sessanta fu il periodo compreso tra il 1961 e il 1965, in cui la Formula 1 fu dedicata e interamente riservata a macchine da corsa con motori fino a 1,5 litri. Questa fase incominciò con una totale dominanza della Ferrari, proseguì con la conquista del Campionato del mondo, ottenuto praticamente all'ultimo secondo, da parte di John Surtees in una vettura con il *cavallino rampante* e la vittoria del Campionato costruttori da parte del marchio rosso stesso nel 1964 e sfociò in una vittoria di Honda all'ultimo giro a Mexico City. Inoltre, suggellò il cambio di guardia dagli italiani negli anni cinquanta (brevemente interrotto dagli anni di egemonia della Mercedes nel 1954 e 1955) agli inglesi. Infine, si caratterizzò per una straordinaria varietà di generi e l'ampiezza quasi democratica del numero di partecipanti: nei cinque anni di durata e 46 Gran Premi, ben 101 piloti circolarono in vetture di 21 marchi diversi.

In vetta erano i soliti favoriti nelle solite vetture a far girare le cose, a meno che non subentrasse un caso fortunato, come la vittoria al debutto di Giancarlo Baghetti al GP de France nel 1961 a Reims. Il pilota più straordinario dell'epoca fu però Jim Clark, anche se numerosi furono coloro che cercarono di mettere i bastoni tra le ruote allo scozzese. Gli anni sessanta fecero emergere sette campioni del mondo. Tra questi l'australiano Jack Brabham, laconico e risoluto nonché un avversario inesorabile sulla pista. È sua la famosissima frase: "When the flag drops, the bullshit stops". Si fidava solo di se stesso, dal 1962 si costruì da solo le sue auto, e nel 1966 vinse il Gran Premio di Reims al volante di una vettura che portava il suo nome.

Poi c'era Phil Hill, che nel 1961 con sole due vittorie stagionali fu il primo americano a entrare nella lista dei campioni, un gentiluomo dall'animo sensibile che una volta giunse tardi all'allenamento, perché aveva voluto ascoltare fino alla fine una messa di Mozart in autoradio. Poi c'era l'omonimo Graham, il baffuto londinese. Dopo aver conquistato il secondo titolo mondiale l'inglese Hill logorò la sua fama e la sua reputazione non riuscendo ad abbandonare questo sport. Nel 1975 finalmente lo fece, e proprio nel novembre di quell'anno si schiantò con l'aereo in un incidente mortale. Un episodio che rasenta l'assurdo. Poi c'era Jim Clark stesso, che ancor'oggi in molti considerano il più grande pilota di tutti i tempi, benché si portasse impresso il marchio indelebile di un semplice pastore scozzese smarrito sul percorso automobilistico.

Ricordiamo poi John Surtees, migrato dallo sport motociclistico, "l'unico campione sulle due e sulle quattro ruote", come veniva ricordato dal pubblico in un cliché stereotipato. Poi ancora il pilota neozelandese Denis Hulme, chiamato "l'orso" che si distingueva per la sua pacatezza stoica e per la sua naturale affidabilità. Ed infine, Jackie Stewart, lo "scozzese volante" numero due in sequenza cronologica. Giunto sesto al suo primo Grand Prix nel gennaio 1965 sul circuito sudafricano di East London, terzo al GP de Monaco cinque mesi dopo, la prima vittoria giunse a Monza nello stesso anno e lo consacrò a successi ben più grandi che giunsero abbondantemente nel 1969, 1971 e 1973 con la triplice conquista del titolo di campione del mondo. La scelta tra i rimanenti è soggettiva. Anch'essi, come alcuni altri, segnarono la Formula 1 degli anni sessanta: il pilota sfortunato Chris Amon, il lungo americano Dan Gurney, dall'aspetto di un vichingo, che sembrava di aver sbagliato secolo, l'audace belga Jacky

Ickx, Bruce McLaren, neozelandesi come Amon e il parimenti dotato, come pilota e come costruttore di macchine da corsa, l'ambizioso Jochen Rindt.

Enzo Ferrari osservava e disprezzava il suo avversario inglese Colin Chapman, fondatore, presidente e direttore operativo della Lotus, definendolo un "assemblatore", come uno, cioè, che partendo da pezzi seriali e pochi altri ingredienti componeva vetture da corsa. Gli anni sessanta approdarono a un duello tra questi due esponenti di filosofie assai diverse: un modo di pensiero che si difendeva in modo risoluto da un lato, e un pensiero ultraprogressivo dall'altro. Le creazioni di Chapman, come la Lotus 25 del 1962 con il suo telaio monoscocca rivoluzionarono la concezione delle corse veloci così come il redditizio lampo di genio di verniciare la livrea del suo parco macchine a partire dal 1968 con i colori variopinti del marchio Gold Leaf, estraneo al mondo automobilistico.

La stagione 1970, per diversi motivi, segnó un cambio di rotta nella storia del Gran Premio, segnando quasi un contrasto rispetto ai dieci anni precedenti. La formula 1 perse Bruce McLaren, Piers Courage e Jochen Rindt tragicamente deceduti, nonché Jack Brabham e Dan Gurney ritiratisi, ma guadagno al contempo giovani talenti come Clay Regazzoni, Emerson Fittipaldi, Ronnie Peterson e François Cevert.

Il fascino è rimasto, ma l'ambientazione è cambiata.

pp. 30/31 *A sermon for the drivers before the Belgian Grand Prix in 1962. Front row: Clark, McLaren, Ireland (holding cigarette), Trintignant (wearing motorbike belt) and de Beaufort. Behind: Maggs, Baghetti, Phil Hill (hidden from view), Siffert, Ricardo Rodriguez, Graham Hill (half hidden), Ginther, Brabham, and others.*

An exceptional line-up: while Graham Hill (BRM) might have been expected to take pole position at the ultra-high speed Ardennes circuit, with perhaps Bruce McLaren (Cooper Climax) front of grid too, the Lotus driver Trevor Taylor's third position was more of a surprise. This was only his fourth grand prix.

Uniform not compulsory: Graham Hill and Bruce McLaren's crash helmets and goggles are as different as the heads they protect. But both faces are filled with determination – and a degree of interest in the photographer.

pp. 36/37 *Genre scene: while Ferrari drivers Ricardo Rodriguez and Phil Hill are battling out a generational conflict at the nightmare Eau Rouge corner, spectators show differing degrees of interest – from fascination to yawns of boredom.*

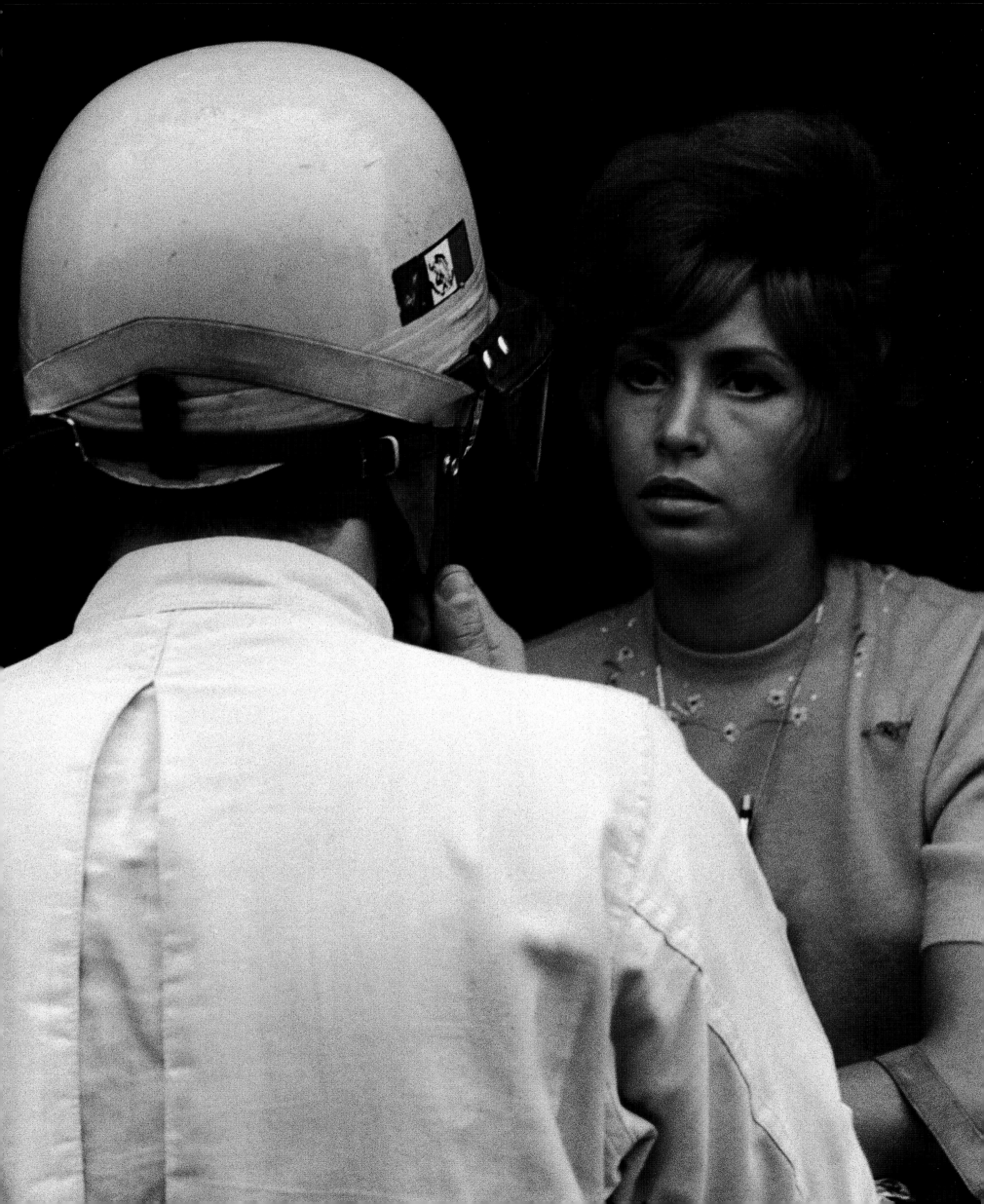

Live fast: while talking to his apprehensive wife, Sara, Ricardo Rodriguez may already be visualizing in his mind's eye the racing line through the endless Burnenville corner. But aged just twenty years, the Mexican had barely half a year left to live.

A game without limits: the end of the sloping pit-lane in the Spa circuit, with only a line of paint to separate it from the track, was intersected directly by the racing line. Today, just as was the case then, the wall of the bridge over the Eau Rouge stream is a lurking threat. Indeed, the name of this stream does not bode well.

Another close shave: at the Blanchimont section of the circuit, Willy Mairesse's Ferrari catches fire after making contact with Trevor Taylor's skidding Lotus and comes off the track. The British man came away with nothing more than shock and a splatter of mud over his racing overalls. The wild Belgian, however, was out of the sport until Monza. John Campbell-Jones can be seen looking over from his Lotus 18 with concern.

Open-air event: on the 5th of August 1962, "The Green Hell" of the Nürburgring was cold and rainy. Dan Gurney (Porsche) was unable to convert his pole position into a win. Right from the start, which was already postponed by an hour, the eventual victor, Graham Hill, managed to keep the upper hand.

Still life with woolly hat, umbrella and a constable: the number 1 on Phil Hill's Ferrari was testament to his title win the previous year. Yet 1962 was a year to forget for the American, and after finding failure in the pouring Eifel rain, he would curse his profession.

A world apart: while Dutch aristocrat Carel Godin de Beaufort wrestles with fate and his
mechanics in his sturdy four-cylinder Porsche nicknamed "Old Fatty Porsche", Jack Brabham
enjoys an ice-lolly.

Tony Maggs looks on while Innes Ireland gets worked up over some problem or other. Masten Gregory, meanwhile, (next to Lorenzo Bandini with his rudimentary form of head protection) is the very image of calm. Both are self-confessed chain smokers, but neither will be fooled by a smoke screen.

pp. 50/51 *Large-scale operation: at the home game in Monza, 1962, Scuderia Ferrari has five cars in the race. Giancarlo Baghetti, seen here inspecting the front end from behind, had to content himself with fifth place behind three English cars and his, then still convalescing, stable mate Mairesse.*

Ladies and gentlemen: the chatter of the three women in the improvised pit in Monaco doesn't appear to have much to do with motor racing. The helmet-clad racers, on the other hand – McLaren, Hall, Taylor, Gurney, Siffert and Ireland – all appear fully focused upon the task in hand.

Never lacking amazement: Jim Clark appears to be astonished by his own artistry in handling the Lotus 25. The Monaco Grand Prix, a city street-circuit left almost in its natural state, never once made it onto the list as one of the Scot's 25 victories.

Side by side: eternal rivals Jim Clark (Lotus no. 9) and Graham Hill (BRM) in Monaco, 1963, approach the Gasometer turn. The harbour is comparatively empty, and the architecture still shows the influence of the Monaco "gingerbread" style.

pp. 58/59 Hands on: at his third attempt and his second time in pole position in the Principality, victory seemed to be beckoning to Clark. But in the 78th lap of 100 the gearbox stopped cooperating. So the Scot assists his civilian helpers in removing the damaged Lotus from the track.

pp. 60/61 *A triumphant smile: the victor was Graham Hill, protected from grasping hands by ropes, cordoned off by the famously efficient Monaco police. This was evidently so agreeable that the moustached hero came back to win it four more times. By the end he was known as the "King of Monaco".*

The woman at his side: Bette Hill (behind is BRM's chief mechanic, Tony Rudd) came to all of her husband's races with a stopwatch, pad of paper and a pencil. Chaos reigned in the run up to the French Grand Prix 1963. Graham is granted a starting position front of grid, although the engine of his BRM 61 has died.

Steaming over: the beginning of the Dutch Grand Prix. The leaders, Jim Clark, Graham Hill and Bruce McLaren, approach "Tarzan", the first right-hand bend. A brisk breeze blows through from the coast. Protection for the spectators is, indeed, more of a token gesture.

Struck dumb: at the start of Reims, the third and fourth lines begin to merge. Innes Ireland protects his mouth and nose with a white strip of fabric, yet still races in a polo shirt just like Joakim Bonnier (no. 44).

pp. 68/69 *In the final phase of the Monaco Grand Prix, 1964, a palm tree casts its long shadow over the car of Lorenzo Bandini. The driver is wearing black gloves. The Ferrari's tyres are covered in white dust from contact with the kerbstones that line the avenues of the Principality.*

Roving reporter: retired grand prix racer Stirling Moss in his blue club blazer reports from the Monaco blue-riband event, setting a precedent for journalists to have the appropriate professional background. Behind, the Grimaldis can be seen heading towards their Rolls-Royce.

pp. 72/73 *Dialogue with a photographer: Dun Gurney in the Brabham-Climax BT7 against the backdrop of the Hôtel de Paris, in Monaco, 1964. The English virtuoso photographer Geoffrey Goddard has just captured the scene on his camera.*

Hurt, but happy: at the Belgian Grand Prix in Spa, 1964, Bruce is hit in the face by a stone. Here he is nevertheless in good spirits because, incredibly, he came in second place behind Jim Clark, despite the fact his Cooper ran down the home straight without fuel, with a lifeless Climax-V8 engine.

Opposite page *Trust in one another: Bruce McLaren and his wife, Pat, in Monaco. The pit is still makeshift and the name spelling leaves something to be desired. But the atmosphere is good. Maybe she just called him "Big Mac"...*

A cumulative effect: Giancarlo Baghetti drives the Scuderia Centro Sud *BRM P57* in Spa as a racing taxi for his crashed colleagues Phil Hill and Bob Anderson. Of course, the air drag coefficient and the top speed of the secondhand red car must have suffered somewhat.

pp. 78/79 *Collective concentration: only a few seconds until the start of the Dutch Grand Prix. John Surtees, that year's world champion, focuses entirely on the race in which he will come second after Clark. He would later own the Ferrari 158 for many years.*

Introversion: sometimes it seemed as if the speedy Scott Jim Clark's gaze and thoughts were entirely directed inwards. His profession and mission required 100% concentration. Even his bitten nails demonstrated the power of his subconscious, as was the case, too, with Alain Prost some time later.

Among his adoring fans: "Le grand vainqueur: Jimmy Clark" called out the track announcer at the end of the 1964 Belgian Grand Prix. This, for once, was an enormous surprise. Gurney and McLaren had been fighting for victory until their fuel ran out, while Graham Hill was sidelined with a defective fuel pump.

pp. 84/85 *Giving it your all: while former grand prix driver Louis Chiron waves in Jo Siffert's Brabham BT11 and Graham Hill's BRM P261 in Monaco, 1965, German photographer Horst Baumann attempts to get the ultimate photo with his Leica camera. Further ahead, the transversally incorporated twelve-cylinder screeches in Richie Ginther's Honda.*

Three-way fight at the station: Lorenzo Bandini and John Surtees force Graham Hill's BRM into a Ferrari sandwich in Monaco. The steel skeleton of the old station provided an ideal place for a makeshift stand, where spectators were protected from straying cars by straw.

Thinking outside the box: next to his wife, Patricia, John Surtees waits for his cue, while this young man already seems to have his eye firmly set upon a future in racing. But not as long as Mum's looking.

A stitch-up: at the Nürburgring, the three times Formula 1 world champion Jackie Stewart sews up a tear in two times champion Graham Hill's racing overalls. The results can be seen – to the astonishment of the women looking on. Racing drivers were just so much more versatile in those days.

Mutual respect: at the French Grand Prix in 1965 in Clermont-Ferrand, the fresh-faced young journalist "Jabby" Crombac introduces Graham Hill to the French Prime Minister Georges Pompidou. Friend of Clark, Crombac was to become one of the most successful and respected Formula 1 writers of his time, regarded as the guild's doyen for many years.

The dress code: before Graham Hill added his own chapter to the seemingly never-ending story of helmet and visor development, he is seen tugging the wristbands of his racing overalls into place. His footwear would have provided very little resistance in high temperatures.

Touching simplicity: in Zandvoort, Richie Ginther's white Honda passes in front of a number of simple billboards, and a group of carefree photographers. Third from the left is John Blunsden, later to become correspondent for the Times, and himself an excellent driver.

Safety concerns: in view of the latent dangers of grand prix racing – demonstrated himself at the wheel of the Brabham in Clermont-Ferrand – Dan Gurney's mouth protection would seem decidedly inadequate.

pp. 100/101 *A flying visit: in Monza, 1965, Jo Siffert, in action for Rob Walker's private team in a Brabham, drops by on John Cooper and his astonishingly young looking driver Jochen Rindt. The Austrian, only just emerging as a top racer, is seen here squatting on the back left wheel of the T77 right before the start.*

The duel of the scots: the Gran Premio d'Italia 1965 brings Jackie Stewart (no. 32) his first Formula 1 victory. He celebrates with his tifosi (fans). Here he is seen approaching the finish line with Jim Clark still providing energetic resistance, remaining in front for 19 laps before his fuel pump left him high and dry.

pp. 104/105 *Car chase: John Surtees in his Ferrari and BRM driver Jackie Stewart, who won this race, herald in the 1966 grand prix season in Monaco. In the apex of the Gasometer turn it is possible to make out the relatively well-protected form of the one-armed German journalist, Dr. Hortolf Biesenberger.*

Personality swap: in Monaco Jim Clark is pictured earnestly discussing serious business with the Beatle, George Harrison: the art of driving in a grand prix. Nevertheless the serious Scot liked to surprise his good friends and acquaintances now and then with his propensity to fool around.

Dry run: before the grand prix begins, Clark gives the Lotus 33 a thorough try out in all its claustrophobic compactness. Ubiquitous, and available from all good car accessory retailers, is the Talbot rear view mirror. Perhaps fans in their Volkswagens have something in common with their idol after all.

Fascinating technology: the view from the slope preceding the crest of the hill before the Massenet left-hand bend allows a glimpse of the complex beauty of the Maserati twelve-cylinder on a fleeing Cooper T81. The setting is, of course, Monaco.

pp. 112/113 *BRM family photo: chief engineer Tony Rudd is pictured with Graham Hill and Jackie Stewart; behind can be seen Bette Hill, and to the right, Helen Stewart. In the middle is Louis "Big Lou" Stanley, in those days still the "speaker" but later to head the team, shown here with his wife, Jean. On the right, the Belgian photographer Eric della Faille looks into shot.*

A matter of view: on the Nürburgring there are more than ten places where cars lose contact with the track. The Nikon on Jackie Stewart's helmet, with its wide-angled lens, is intended to give an idea of the view from the cockpit.

For the love of corners: the Tarzan bend in Zandvoort tempts even former champion
Jack Brabham – far from still being a juvenile daredevil – into wonderfully controlled
drifts. Moment by moment and point by point, the Australian was drawing closer to his
third title, in 1966.

Bubbly with delight: at the Brands Hatch circuit, 100 bottles of champagne were kept as a reward for the fastest times in practice. For Brabham this was the elixir of life and his motivation: the very next day he claimed victory at the bumpy Kent circuit, recording the fastest lap.

Back-four: at two o'clock on the dot, the German Automobile Club AvD's baron Leo von Diergardt unfurls the starter flag for the German Grand Prix. John Surtees, having switched from Ferrari to Cooper-Maserati only four races previously, claims himself a small advantage ahead of the fastest qualifier, Clark.

Role reversal: at the Monza Gran Premio d'Italia, Clark leaps out of his Lotus 43 with its noisy and complex H16 rear engine from BRM and straight into a Lotus-Miniature – to the delight of its young owner.

pp. 124/125 *Racing soldier: of slight build and a stranger to any kind of body art, Jochen Rindt could almost have stood as a sculpture model for the Christian martyr Sebastian – minus the arrows. His face, however, betrays his steely resolve and unflinching determination.*

Park and ride: Jo Siffert had to work his way up from nothing in motor sport, and never lost sight of his humble origins. Therefore the Swiss racer took up every offer of a lift, with Innes Ireland in 1964 in Spa, and on Graham Hill's Lotus in Monaco 1967.

Two-faced: just how his compatriots loved him: golden boy Lorenzo Bandini, smiling, with a colourful neckerchief. On the 7th of May 1967, however, he seemed to suspect what the future had in store. An accident resulting in a fire in the 82nd lap led to his final defeat in the fight against Death, three days later.

Leave time to do its work: victory in Monaco didn't bring joy to Dennis Hulme, even less so because Bandini had never been able to finish his pursuit of him. Four months later Margherita, the widow of the deceased, resplendently congratulates John Surtees on his Honda success in Monza.

As the elite squad – Graham Hill and Jim Clark – kick back shirtless in the sun during a break in practice, there is a more formal dress code at the presentation of the new DFV engine in Zandvoort, 1967. DFV creator Keith Duckworth, seen next to the head of the Lotus team, Colin Chapman, in both photographs, never liked to be caught without a tie.

133

A highly successful debut: Lotus star driver Jim Clark trailed by previous year's champion Jack Brabham, both seen here lapping Jo Siffert in Rob Walker's Cooper-Maserati, in Zandvoort. The Scot eventually won in the first triumph for the Lotus 49; an ideal way to end the first day for Ford's brand new product, the DFV.

pp. 136/137 *Crowned and unscathed: despite minor problems with the brakes, clutch, accelerator and gearbox Clark nonetheless crosses the finish line. The Lotus, however, did slightly stray out during the slowdown lap, a fact given away by the disintegrated straw bale clinging to the hot tyres.*

Setting the scene: two years separate both these photos of Bruce McLaren, in 1965 perched on the rear wheel of his Cooper-Climax in Clermont-Ferrand, and in 1967 in Le Mans, flanked by Goodyear Girls. This was the beginning of the trend for uniformed, attractive girls to ornament the paddock.

Reason to celebrate: the Bugatti circuit in Le Mans was nicknamed a "Micky Mouse" sort of circuit by Jack Brabham. Nevertheless, he is seen here to be enjoying his victory, the Esso Tiger in his arm and his helmet still on, such was his haste. That sparkling beverage is being savoured out of wine glasses.

141

pp. 142/143 *An island battle scene: Chris Amon, in the only Ferrari in the race, is hot on the heels of Jack Brabham through Copse Corner at Silverstone. The Australian's car was known to be the "widest" in the sport, and the New Zealander's ability to overtake him was reduced even further when the rear view mirror of Brabham's Brabham was shaken off during the race. Only a knee-high wall protected racing cars and photographers from each other.*

An accident in the pit lane: during practice for the British GP, a part of Hill's rear suspension became detached, the Lotus crashing into the wall. A wheel was sheared off while the monocoque and radiator were both damaged. This means a lot of work in store for the team that night. Colin Chapman and mechanic Jim Endruweit (in the Firestone jacket) look on, dismayed.

Always a smile on his lips: shortly before the start, Jackie Stewart jokes with colleagues despite the fact that the H16 engine in his BRM gives him little reason to be cheerful. The question of safety, energetically promoted by the Scot himself, is already beginning to gain ground.

pp. 148/149 *Unready for take-off: the cars are still coming out of their bays before the start of the British Grand Prix. This is the only reason why Jim Clark, with the fastest practice time, finds himself next to Guy Ligier in his Repco-Brabham. The frenchman's recorded time was nine seconds slower than the Scot's.*

The centre of attention: this was the second win of the season for Clark, at Silverstone. On the right, Keith Duckworth and Colin Chapman applaud. The trophy's beauty was not universally acknowledged – and the women behind, in their glass-paned isolation, clearly think they can see why.

One giant leap: the winner at the Nürburgring is Denny Hulme, who was to be that year's world champion in his Repco-Brabham. The car was just like the driver – perhaps not the fastest but certainly the most reliable, well and truly down to earth.

Distant affection: in Monza, the women look on at events on the race track with something of a weary eye, enjoying the timid early autumn rays of sun. Chris Amon's helmet sits in striking contrast.

Five men and a motor: the BRM V12 of Bruce McLaren's McLaren needs work. Enzo Ferrari
is therefore able to absorb all the attention himself on one of his rare appearances in Monza.
Even head technician Mauro Forghieri (in glasses) falls comparatively into the background.

The punch line: John Surtees only leads for one lap at the Italian GP, seen here being trailed by McLaren, Amon and Rindt as they approach the Parabolica corner in Monza. But it is the last lap and therefore the one that counts. Critics jeeringly nicknamed his lightweight Honda "Hondola" because it contained parts originating from Lola.

Spot the difference: Jackie Stewart at the Italian Grand Prix in 1966, and in 1967 on exactly the same spot, in the BRM with its refractory H16 engine at the rear. Also appearing in both photos is its maker, Tony Rudd (in glasses).

pp. 166/167 *Hidden temptations: as Lucien Bianchi begins to brake at Mirabeau, he must surely catch a glimpse of these tempting invitations to a Monaco nightclub in the rear view mirror of his Cooper-BRM. It's only the most important triviality in the world – after Formula 1, of course.*

Burnt out: in the 17th lap of the Monaco Grand Prix, 1968, Pedro Rodriguez has had an accident leaving the Mirabeau sector, probably because of a broken drive shaft cutting through a brake pipe. A small fire was promptly extinguished. McLaren driver Hulme barely gives the body of the car, lying at the side of the road, so much as a second glance.

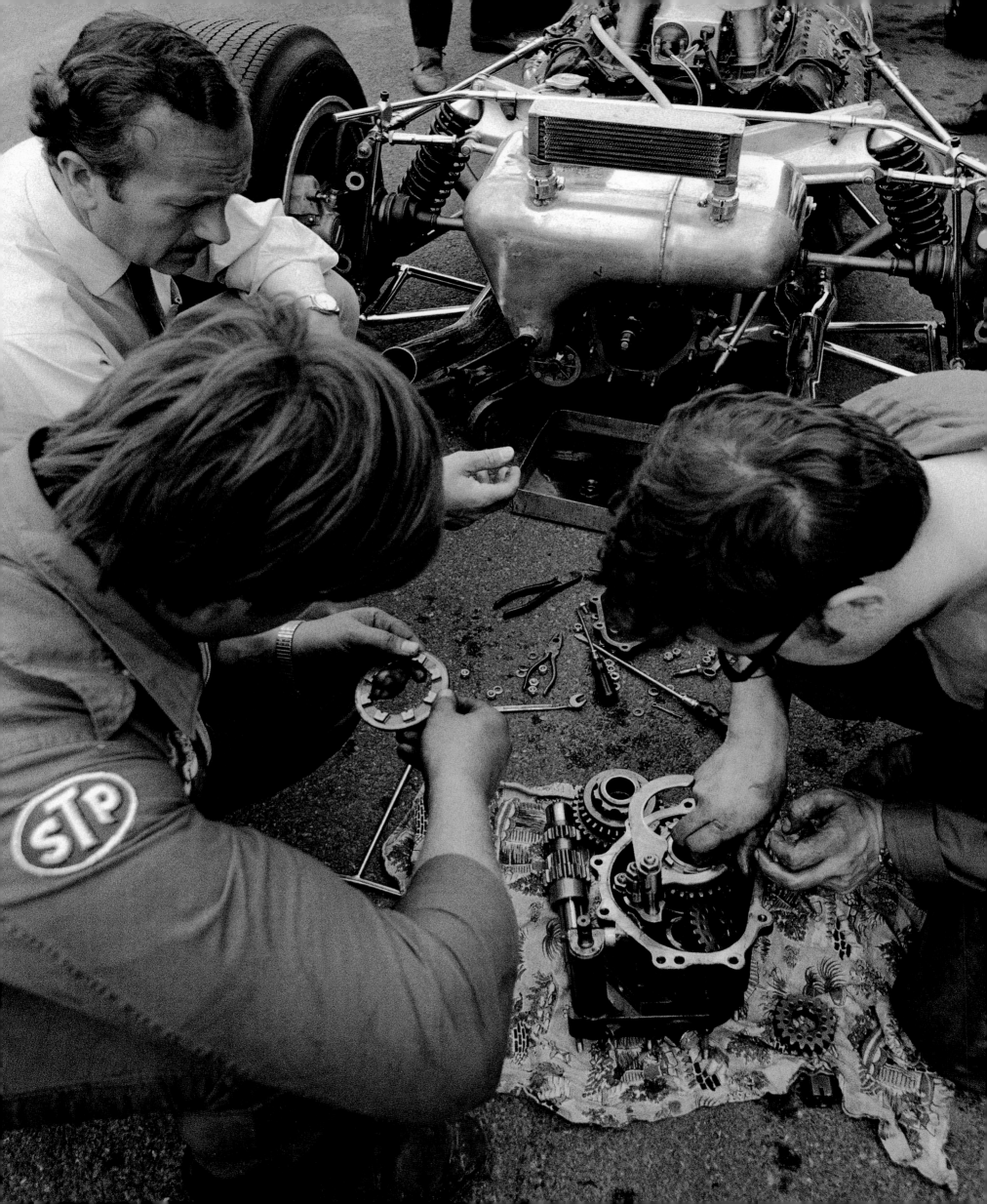

pp. 170/171 *Multiple uses: mounted on delicate poles, the wing of a Ferrari 312 serves as an all-purpose placement area for the well-qualified experts of Scuderia, here in Spa.*

A jack of all trades: one minute Colin Chapman is supervising work on a gear box, the next he is spellbound following the much more dynamic action on the track. Racer's wife Bette Hill sits behind him. Both scenes are of a poignant simplicity.

A brief moment of contemplation: in Spa, Bruce McLaren has just won his fourth and final
grand prix title – this time in a car bearing his own name. Pedro Rodriguez and Jacky Ickx,
in second and third place, also appear somewhat contemplative.

Unwelcome advances: Jacky Ickx has his hands full in the rainy Dutch GP at the Hunzerug corner, trying to regain control of his Ferrari. Jean-Pierre Beltoise and his Matra V12, on the other hand, are heading firmly in the right direction – to the right.

pp. 178/179 *Open visor: the Stewarts celebrate Jackie's win in Zandvoort, in an oasis of intimacy. Sympathetic assistance is required as the Scot's right hand is bandaged up with a partially fractured wrist. This made his success, more than 90 seconds ahead of his Matra team mate Jean-Pierre Beltoise in second place, all the more astonishing.*

Reading out the riot act: Misters Surtees, Brabham, Stewart, Rodriguez and Siffert once again have the rules of the game hammered into them, in Rouen. On the left, next to Surtees, Jean-Marie Balestre – president of the Automobile Associations FFSA, FISA and FIA, from 1978 to 1996 – also listens attentively.

pp. 182/183 *A helping hand: Jo Siffert's visor repeatedly steams up during the French GP. He stops close to Graham Hill's Lotus, out of the race with a damaged drive shaft, to borrow his. In the background Surtees is seen defying the aqua-inferno in his Honda.*

A good mood all round: Hahne (standing on the left), Beltoise, Courage, Oliver, Siffert and Hill, as well as the two Belgians, Bianchi and Ickx, in the background, seem little bothered by the chicanery of the weather in the Eifel. Having come fifth in training, Cooper pilot Vic Elford can even be seen fooling around.

pp. 186/187 *The grey-green hell: on days like this, the 4th of August 1968, at the Nürburgring, brave men have become heroes. Here Jo Siffert, in his dark blue Lotus from Rob Walker's private racing team, is seen inside the right-hand bend preceding the Karussell.*

Champions League: the Monza tifosi show a disregard for risk, fashioning their own peep-hole boxes as the need arises. A few hundred metres further on, Vic Elford's Cooper-BRM is "guarded" following an accident on the fourth lap. It would probably be a bit awkward to carry home as a souvenir.

Air resistance: Jack Brabham, seen on the right in conversation with designer Ron Tauranac, uses the Autodromo Nazionale di Monza as a laboratory for all types of aerodynamic technology.

Signs of the past: John Surtees is this time unable to convert his pole position in Monza, his winged Honda in front of McLaren, Ickx and Rindt, into a win. Denny Hulme's success nevertheless gets things fired up as might be expected. All this fascist bombast is reminiscent of Mussolini's era.

193

The King of Monaco: in the third race of the 1969 season, Graham Hill speeds towards his fifth victory in the Principality. Denny Hulme, meanwhile, here on the left-hand Massenet corner, must content himself with sixth place. The safety of photographers and racing officials still leaves something to be desired, however.

Hanging around: Innes Ireland, having become a fully fledged member of the writers' guild and ever-ready to play a prank, falls through his chair at a meeting of the journalists' association IRPA. The IRPA secretary Adriano Cimarosti looks down at the wreckage, amused. In a racing car, however, Ireland was not one to take a joke.

Town life, country life: the Monaco GP has been a classic, carved-in-stone date on the racing calendar ever since the Principality opened its doors to the sport in 1929. The Circuit de Charade in Clermont-Ferrand was home only to four Formula 1 guest performances, between 1965 and 1972. Here Jacky Ickx is seen in his Brabham, in front of Lotus driver, Rindt. The year is 1969.

pp. 200/201 *Alcohol abuse: without a doubt, Jackie Stewart knew best how to handle a Formula 1 car. As for being able to handle his champagne, it looks a little like it might have gone down the wrong way.*

British noblesse: having been out basking among their adoring fans, the first three of the French GP – Jackie Stewart, Jean-Pierre Beltoise and Jack Ickx – go out into their public in a Rolls-Royce. The young women appear to be enjoying the drive, too.

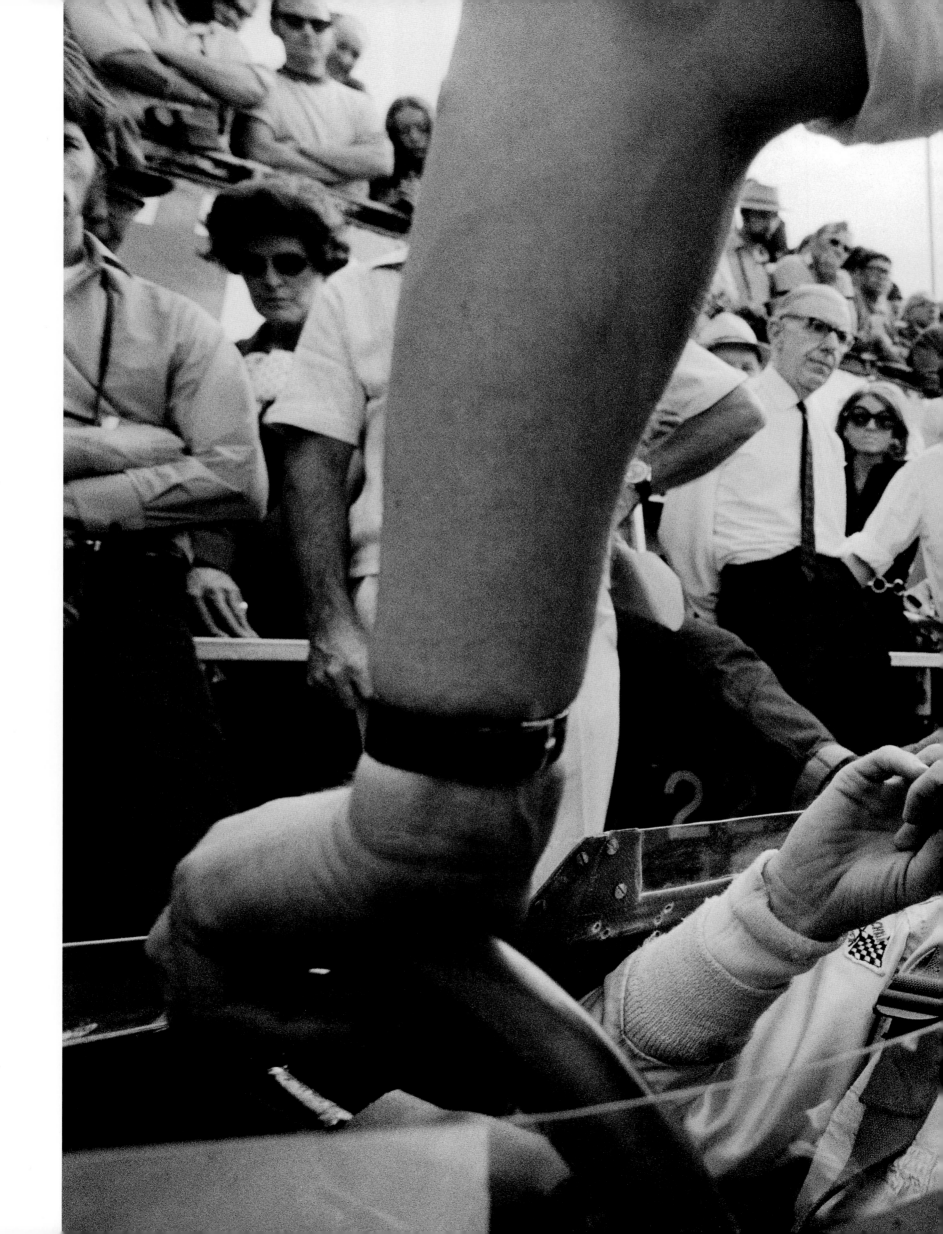

204

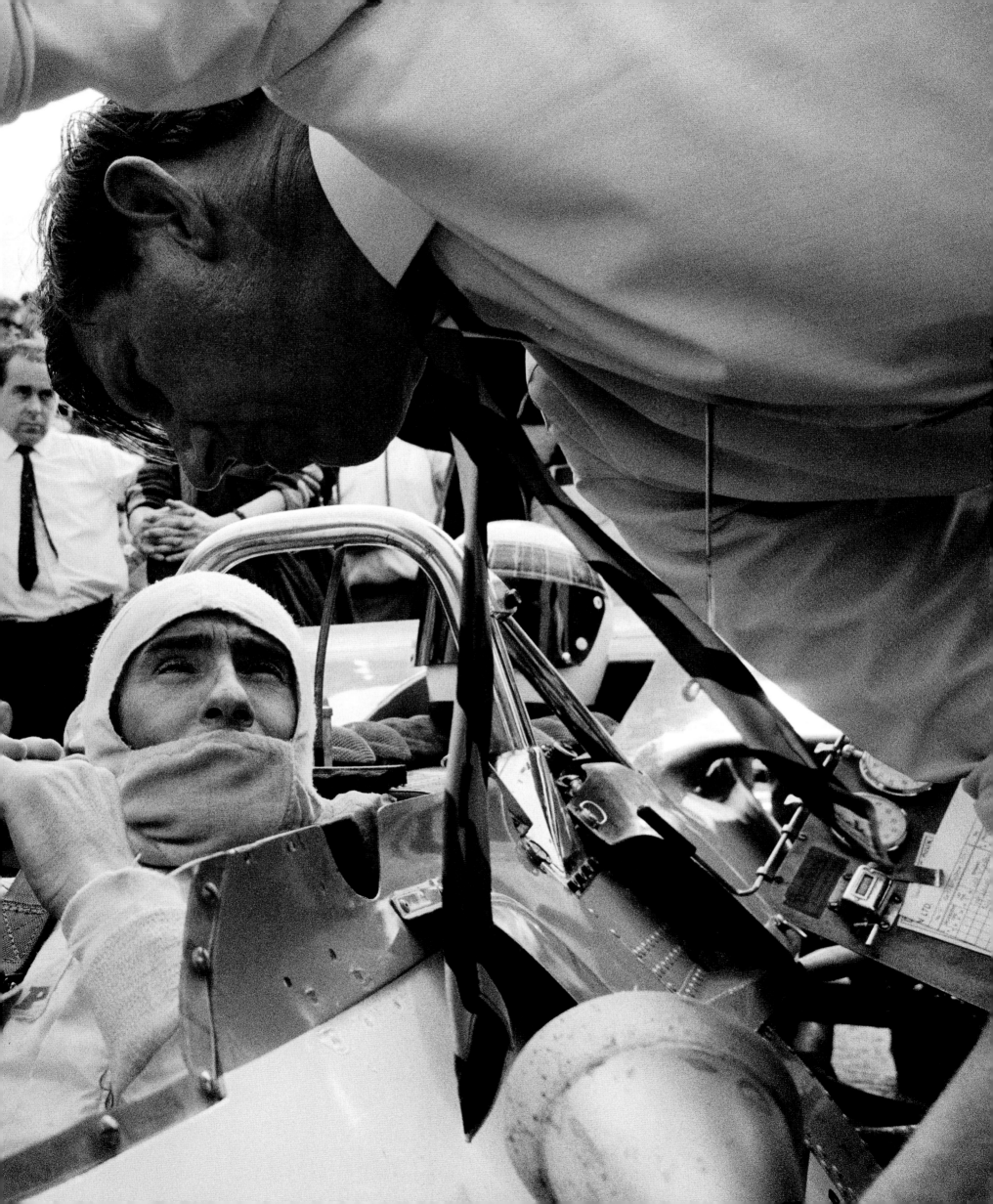

pp. 204/205 *A master and a model student: Jackie Stewart and his employer, Ken Tyrrell, at the British Grand Prix. The Scot's win, his fifth of the season, was another step on the path towards his first title.*

Not without Helen: for this victory at Silverstone he had first to be pitted against friend and rival Jochen Rindt, and it tasted all the sweeter for it – surely just like the contents of the two decanters filled with VAT 69, which Stewart would later be presented with by representatives of the Scottish whisky distillery William Sanderson.

Forest flight: for a second, Jackie Stewart's Matra MS80 gives the tyres a break while practising for the German Grand Prix at the Nürburgring – the last use of the old circuit with all its bumps and ruts. It's a dangerous sport …

Looking forwards, looking back: at the junction between decades, Jacky Ickx looks back over the last ten years filled with triumph and tragedy. But the Belgian, still young, was to span both eras. The very next day he would claim the German Grand Prix as his second GP win. He was standing on the threshold of a career that was to be filled with superlatives: runner-up in the championship that year and the next, and king of the long endurance race, with no fewer than six wins in Le Mans.

Index

Rainer W. Schlegelmilch

Rainer W. Schlegelmilch saw his first race in 1962, when he was photographing a series of portraits at the Nürburgring 1000 kilometres for his final examination at the Bavarian State School of Photography in Munich. Eighteen months later, he opened his own photo design studio in Frankfurt, yet motor racing always remained a major aspect of his work. Right from the very beginning, initially in monochrome only, he was the photographer for numerous prestigious motor sport publications. Since 1974 he has focused exclusively on Formula 1. From the nineties up to the present-day he has published over 20 works of photography which have brought him worldwide acclaim. Today, his photo archives total 15,000 monochrome photographs and over 400,000 colour slides and digital images. Even after more than 500 GPs he is still driven by the same passion: that never-ending quest for an even more perfect photo.

Sein erstes Rennen sah Rainer W. Schlegelmilch 1962, als er eine Reihe von Porträts beim 1000-km-Rennen auf dem Nürburgring für sein Examen an der damaligen Bayerischen Staatslehranstalt für Photographie in München aufnahm. 18 Monate später eröffnete er sein Studio für Fotodesign in Frankfurt. Der Rennsport blieb jedoch weiterhin ein wichtiger Aspekt seiner Arbeit. Schlegelmilch fotografierte seit Beginn seiner Karriere für zahlreiche renommierte Motorsport-Publikationen, anfangs ausschließlich in Schwarz-Weiß. Er konzentrierte sich ab 1974 einzig und allein auf die Formel 1. Von den neunziger Jahren bis heute hat er mehr als 20 Bildbände veröffentlicht, die ihm weltweit das Lob der Kritiker einbrachten. Sein Foto-Archiv umfasst heute insgesamt 15 000 Schwarz-Weiß-Fotografien und über 400 000 Farbdias und digitale Bilder. Selbst nach weit über 500 Grands Prix brennt in ihm noch immer dieselbe Leidenschaft: die nicht endende Suche nach einem noch besseren Foto.

Rainer W. Schlegelmilch a vu sa première course en 1962, au cours de laquelle il pris une série de portraits lors des 1000 kilomètres de Nürburgring pour son examen final de l'École de photographie de Bavière. 18 mois plus tard, il a ouvert son studio de design photographique à Francfort; mais la course automobile est toujours resté un aspect majeur de son oeuvre. Dès le début, tout d'abord en noir et blanc, il a photographié pour de nombreuses et prestigieuses publications automobiles. Depuis 1974, il s'est exclusivement consacré aux Grands Prix de Formule 1. Des années quatre-vingt-dix à aujourd'hui, il a publié plus de vingt ouvrages photographiques, qui lui ont apporté un grand succès au niveau mondial. Aujourd'hui, ses archives photographiques comptent un total de 15 000 photographies en noir et blanc et plus de 400 000 clichés couleurs et images digitales. Même après 500 Grands Prix, la même passion rugit toujours en lui: celle de la quête perpétuelle d'une photo toujours meilleure.

Rainer W. Schlegelmilch presenció su primera carrera en 1962, cuando realizó una serie de retratos en los 1000 km de Nürburgring para su exámen final en la Escuela Pública de Fotografía de Bavaria, en Munich. Un año y medio después abrió su estudio de diseño fotográfico en Fráncfort; no obstante, las carreras siempre han sido un aspecto fundamental de su trabajo. Desde el comienzo mismo tomó instantáneas, inicialmente monocromáticas, para numerosas publicaciones de gran prestigio relacionadas con el mundo del motor. Desde 1974 se concentró exclusivamente en los Grandes Premios de Fórmula 1. Entre 1990 y nuestros días, ha publicado más de 20 trabajos de fotografía, los cuales le han reportado reconocimiento internacional. Hoy, sus archivos comprenden 15 000 fotografías en blanco y negro y más de 400 000 diapositivas en color e imágenes digitales. Incluso tras 500 Grandes Premios sigue estando impulsado por la misma pasión: La interminable búsqueda de una foto aún mejor.

Rainer W. Schlegelmilch assistette alla sua prima gara nel 1962, realizzando una serie di ritratti alla 1000 km di Nürburgring per il suo esame finale alla Scuola di Fotografia di Monaco di Baviera. Diciotto mesi più tardi aprì il suo studio di design fotografico a Francoforte, ma le corse automobilistiche avrebbero sempre rappresentato uno degli aspetti più importanti del suo lavoro. Fin dagli esordi della sua carriera, inizialmente votata al solo bianco e nero, Schlegelmilch ha fotografato per molte prestigiose pubblicazioni dedicate agli sport motoristici. A partire dal 1974 si è concentrato esclusivamente sulle gare automobilistiche della Formula 1. Dagli anni novanta a oggi ha pubblicato più di 20 opere fotografiche, che lo hanno consacrato al successo internazionale. A tutt'oggi i suoi archivi contano 15 000 scatti in bianco e nero e più di 400 000 tra diapositive a colori e immagini digitali. E anche dopo 500 Gran Premi, la passione che lo spinge è la stessa di sempre: la ricerca incessante di uno scatto ancora più geniale.

Acknowledgements

Firstly, I would like to thank my publisher, Hendrik teNeues, for having given me the opportunity to put together this collection of photographs from the black and white shots I took in the sixties – Formula 1's greatest era. I wish to thank my friend Hartmut Lehbrink, to whom I am indebted for writing such perfect accompanying texts; the publishing team, Dieter Haberzettl, Axel Theyhsen, Robert Kuhlendahl and Pit Pauen, for an effective collaboration, and Stefano Luzzatto for all the understanding he showed during the scanning process. I must also thank my long-time companion, Jackie Stewart, for writing the foreword, as well as Wolfgang Momberger, a friend who, with his passion for motor sports, has provided constant motivation.

Imprint

© 2010 teNeues Verlag GmbH + Co. KG, Kempen
Photographs © 2010 Rainer W. Schlegelmilch. All rights reserved.

Foreword by Sir Jackie Stewart
Introduction and captions by Hartmut Lehbrink
Translations by RR Communications:
English: Zoë Cecilia Brasier, Romina Russo
German: Bianca Dett, Romina Russo
French: Matt Cauquil, Romina Russo
Spanish: Bruno Plaza, Romina Russo
Italian: Alessia Viola, Romina Russo
Design by Axel Theyhsen, Robert Kuhlendahl
Editorial coordination by Pit Pauen
Production by Dieter Haberzettl
Drum scans by Stefano Luzzatto
Color separation by ORT Medienverbund

Published by teNeues Publishing Group

teNeues Verlag GmbH + Co. KG
Am Selder 37, 47906 Kempen, Germany
Phone: 0049-2152-916-0
Fax: 0049-2152-916-111
e-mail: books@teneues.de

Press department: Andrea Rehn
Phone: 0049-2152-916-202
e-mail: arehn@teneues.de

teNeues Publishing Company
7 West 18th Street, New York, NY 10011, USA
Phone: 001-212-627-9090
Fax: 001-212-627-9511

teNeues Publishing UK Ltd.
21 Marlowe Court, Lymer Avenue, London SE19 1LP, Great Britain
Phone: 0044-208-670-7522
Fax: 0044-208-670-7523

teNeues France S.A.R.L.
39, rue des Billets, 18250 Henrichemont, France
Phone: 0033-2-4826-9348
Fax: 0033-1-7072-3482

www.teneues.com

ISBN 978-3-8327-9436-1

Printed in Italy

Bibliographic information published by the
Deutsche Nationalbibliothek. The Deutsche Nationalbibliothek
lists this publication in the Deutsche Nationalbibliografie;
detailed bibliographic data are available in the Internet
at http://dnb.d-nb.de.

teNeues Publishing Group

Kempen
Cologne
Düsseldorf
Hamburg
London
Munich
New York
Paris

teNeues